PRESENTED TO:

_____

BY:

_____

DATE:

_____

HOPE

F·O·R

EVERYDAY
LIVING

365 DEVOTIONS

CRISWELL FREEMAN

Scripture quotations are taken from:

The Holy Bible, King James Version

The Holy Bible, New International Version (NIV) Copyright © 1973, 1978, 1984, by International Bible Society. Used by permission of Zondervan Publishing House. All rights reserved.

The Holy Bible, New King James Version (NKJV) Copyright © 1982 by Thomas Nelson, Inc. Used by permission.

New Century Version (NCV) © 1987, 1988, 1991 by Word Publishing, a division of Thomas Nelson, Inc. All rights reserved. Used by permission.

Cover Design by Karen Phillips
Page Layout by Bart Dawson

1-4041-8591-7

Printed in the United States of America

INTRODUCTION

We live in a world where hope is often in short supply. When we focus too intently on the media's avalanche of negative news—or when we become too wrapped up in the inevitable demands and disappointments of everyday life—we can easily fall prey to the pessimism that seems to permeate 21st-Century life. But when we focus, instead, on the timeless promises found in God's Holy Word, we are reminded that hope can—and should—belong to all men and women who are wise enough to entrust their futures to God.

Today and every day, the sun rises upon a world filled with God's presence and His love. As believing Christians, we have so many reasons to be hopeful: The Father is in His heaven, His love is everlasting, and we, His children, are blessed beyond measure. Yet sometimes we find ourselves distracted by the demands, the frustrations, and the uncertainties of daily life. But even during our darkest days, God never leaves us for an instant. And even when our hopes are dimmed, God's light still shines brightly. As followers of God's Son, we are called to search for that light—and to keep searching for it as long as we live.

This text contains 365 devotional readings that are intended to point you towards God's light by lifting your spirits, lowering your anxieties, raising your hopes, and strengthening your faith. As you read these passages, take time to contemplate your own circumstances, and remember this: Whatever the size of your challenges, God is bigger. Much bigger.

God will instruct you, protect you, energize you, and heal you . . . if you let Him. So pray fervently, listen carefully, work diligently, and hope mightily. Do your best and trust God with the rest. Then, you can rest assured: whatever "it" is, God can handle it . . . and will.

HOPE FOR EVERYDAY LIVING

*I wait for the Lord, my soul waits, And in His word
I do hope. My soul waits for the Lord
More than those who watch for the morning—
Yes, more than those who watch for the morning.*

Psalm 130:5-6 NKJV

☞ When hope seems to be in short supply, there is a source to which we can turn in order to restore our perspective and our strength. That source is God. When we lift our prayers to the Creator, we avail ourselves of God's power, God's wisdom, and God's love. And when we allow God's Son to reign over our hearts, we are transformed, not just for a day, but for all eternity.

Are you looking for a renewed sense of hope? If so, it's time to place your future in the loving hands of God's only begotten Son. When you do, you'll discover that hope is not only highly perishable, but that it is also readily renewable . . . one day—and one moment—at a time.

☞ *Like the winds of the sea are the ways of fate as we voyage through our life. Tis the set of the soul that decides the goal and not the storm or the strife.*

Ella Wheeler Wilcox

GROWING WISE

You are my hope, O Lord God;
You are my trust from my youth.

Psalm 71:5 NKJV

❧ Wisdom and hope are traveling companions. Wise men and women learn to think optimistically about their lives, their futures, and their faith. The pessimists, however, are not so fortunate; they choose instead to focus their thoughts and energies on faultfinding, criticizing, and complaining, with precious little to show for their efforts.

To become wise, we must seek God's wisdom—the wisdom of hope—and we must live according to God's Word. To become wise, we must seek God's guidance with consistency and purpose. To become wise, we must not only learn the lessons of life, we must live by them.

Do you seek wisdom for yourself and for your family? Then remember this: The ultimate source of wisdom is the Word of God. When you study God's Word and live according to His commandments, you will grow wise, you will remain hopeful, and you will be a blessing to your family and to the world.

❧ *Wisdom is knowledge applied. Head knowledge is useless on the battlefield. Knowledge stamped on the heart makes one wise.*

Beth Moore

LIVING ON PURPOSE

Whatever you do, do all to the glory of God.

1 Corinthians 10:31 NKJV

☞ Life is best lived on purpose. And purpose, like everything else in the universe, begins with God. Whether you realize it or not, God has a plan for your life, a divine calling, a direction in which He is leading you. When you welcome God into your heart and establish a genuine relationship with Him, He will begin, in time, to make His purposes known.

Sometimes, God's intentions will be clear to you; other times, God's plan will seem uncertain at best. But even on those difficult days when you are unsure which way to turn, you must never lose sight of these overriding facts: God created you for a reason; He has important work for you to do; and He's waiting patiently for you to do it.

And the next step is up to you.

☞ *If the Lord calls you, He will equip you for the task He wants you to fulfill.*

Warren Wiersbe

☞ *There is a path before you that you alone can walk. There is a purpose that you alone can fulfill.*

Karla Dornacher

WORSHIP HIM

*For it is written, "You shall worship the Lord your God,
and Him only you shall serve."*

Matthew 4:10 NKJV

☞ The more intently you worship God, the more
likely you are to remain a hope-filled believer. When
you choose to worhsip the Father sincerely and
often, you reap a plentiful harvest of joy, peace, and
abundance. But if you distance yourself from God by
foolishly worshipping earthly possessions or personal
gratification, you'll be making a mistake of profound
proportions.

Have you accepted the grace of God's only
begotten Son? Then worship Him. Worship Him
today and every day. Worship Him with sincerity and
thanksgiving. Write His name on your heart and rest
assured that He, too, has written your name on His.

☞ *Worship is about rekindling an ashen heart into a
blazing fire.*

Liz Curtis Higgs

☞ *In commanding us to glorify Him, God is inviting us
to enjoy Him.*

C. S. Lewis

THE SHEPHERD'S GIFT

*My cup runs over. Surely goodness and mercy shall
follow me all the days of my life; and I will dwell
in the house of the Lord forever.*

Psalm 23:5-6 NKJV

☞ The Word of God is clear: Christ came in order
that we might have life abundant and life eternal.
Eternal life is a priceless possession of all who invite
Christ into their hearts, but God's abundance is
optional: He does not force it upon us.

When we entrust our hearts and our days to
the One who created us, we experience abundance
through the grace and sacrifice of His Son. But, when
we turn our thoughts and direct our energies away
from God's commandments, we inevitably forfeit the
spiritual abundance that might otherwise be ours.

Do you sincerely seek the riches that our Savior
offers to those who give themselves to Him? Then
follow Him completely and obey Him without
reservation. When you do, you will receive the love
and the abundance that He has promised. Seek first
the salvation that is available through a personal
relationship with Jesus Christ, and then claim the
joy, the peace, and the spiritual abundance that the
Shepherd offers His sheep.

☞ *People, places, and things were never meant to give us
life. God alone is the author of a fulfilling life.*

Gary Smalley & John Trent

IN TIMES OF ADVERSITY

For whatever is born of God overcomes the world.
And this is the victory that has overcome
the world—our faith.

1 John 5:4 NKJV

☞ All of us face times of adversity. On occasion, we all must endure the disappointments and tragedies that befall believers and nonbelievers alike. The reassuring words of 1 John 5:4 remind us that when we accept God's grace, we overcome the passing hardships of this world by relying upon His strength, His love, and His promise of eternal life.

When we call upon God in heartfelt prayer, He will answer—in His own time and according to His own plan—and He will heal us. And while we are waiting for God's plans to unfold and for His healing touch to restore us, we can be comforted in the knowledge that our Creator will and can overcome any obstacle, even if we cannot. Let us take God at His word, let us trust Him, and let us have hope for today, for tomorrow, and for eternity.

☞ *Adversity is always unexpected and unwelcomed. It is an intruder and a thief, and yet in the hands of God, adversity becomes the means through which His supernatural power is demonstrated.*

Charles Stanley

CONTAGIOUS FAITH

Now the just shall live by faith.

Hebrews 10:38 NKJV

☞ Hope, like enthusiastic Christianity, is contagious. If you enjoy a hope-filled, life-altering relationship with God, that relationship will have an impact on others—perhaps a profound impact.

Are you genuinely excited about your faith and your future? And do you make your enthusiasm known to those around you? Or are you a "silent ambassador" for Christ? God's preference is clear: He intends that you stand before others and proclaim your faith.

Does Christ reign over your life? If so, then it's time to share your testimony, your hopes, and your enthusiasm. The world needs all three.

☞ *Enthusiasm, like the flu, is contagious—we get it from one another.*

Barbara Johnson

☞ *There seems to be a chilling fear of holy enthusiasm among the people of God. We try to tell how happy we are—but we remain so well-controlled that there are very few waves of glory experienced in our midst.*

A. W. Tozer

LOOKING GOOD . . . TO WHOM?

As for myself, I do not care if I am judged by you or by any human court. I do not even judge myself. I know of no wrong I have done, but this does not make me right before the Lord. The Lord is the One who judges me.

1 Corinthians 4:3-4 NCV

☞ If you're like most people, you seek the admiration of your neighbors, your coworkers, and your family members. But the eagerness to please others should never overshadow your eagerness to please God. If you seek to fulfill the purposes that God has in store for you, then you must be a "doer of the word." And how can you do so? By putting God first.

Martin Luther issued this stern warning: "You may as well quit reading and hearing the Word of God and give it to the devil if you do not desire to live according to it." Luther understood that obedience leads to abundance just as surely as disobedience leads to disaster; you should understand it, too.

Would you like a time-tested formula for successful living? Here it is: Don't just listen to God's Word, live by it. Does this sound too simple? Perhaps it is simple, but it is also the only way to reap the marvelous riches that God has in store for you.

☞ *There may be no trumpet sound or loud applause when we make a right decision, just a calm sense of resolution and peace.*

Gloria Gaither

YOU ARE BLESSED

I will make them and the places all around My hill a blessing; and I will cause showers to come down in their season; there shall be showers of blessing.

Ezekiel 34:26 NKJV

☞ If you were to sit down and began counting your blessings, how long would it take? A very, very long time indeed. Your blessings include life, freedom, family, friends, talents, and possessions, for starters. But, your greatest blessing—a gift that is yours for the asking—is God's gift of salvation through Christ Jesus.

Today, why not take a pencil and paper and begin making a list of your blessings? You most certainly will not be able to make a complete list, but take a few moments and jot down as many blessings as you can. Then give thanks to the giver of all good things: God. His love for you is eternal, as are His gifts. And it's never too soon—or too late—to offer Him thanks.

☞ *I discovered that sorrow was not to be feared but rather endured with hope and expectancy that God would use it to visit and bless my life.*

Jill Briscoe

☞ *God wants his people to earnestly seek his will and to pray for it, and thus to become agents of the blessing God brings.*

James Montgomery Boice

CHARACTER COUNTS

But also for this very reason, giving all diligence,
add to your faith virtue, to virtue knowledge.

2 Peter 1:5 NKJV

☞ The Bible makes it clear that God rewards integrity just as surely as He punishes duplicity. So, if we seek to earn the kind of lasting rewards that God bestows upon those who obey His commandments, we must make honesty the hallmark of our dealings with others.

Character is built slowly over a lifetime. Character is the sum of every right decision, every honest word, every noble thought, and every heartfelt prayer. It is built upon a foundation of industry, generosity, and humility. Character is a precious thing—difficult to build but easy to tear down. As believers in Christ, we must seek to live each day with discipline, honesty, and faith. When we do, integrity becomes a habit. And God smiles.

☞ *Character is formed by doing the thing we are supposed to do, when it should be done, whether we feel like doing it or not.*

Father Flanagan

☞ *Character cannot be developed in ease and quiet. Only through experience of trial and suffering can the soul be strengthened, vision cleared, ambition inspired, and success achieved.*

Helen Keller

CHOOSING TO CONTROL MYSELF

So prepare your minds for service and have self-control.

1 Peter 1:13 NCV

☞ God's Word reminds us again and again that our Creator expects us to lead disciplined lives. God doesn't reward laziness, misbehavior, or apathy. To the contrary, He expects believers to behave with dignity and discipline.

We live in a world in which leisure is glorified and indifference is often glamorized. But God has other plans. He did not create us for lives of mediocrity; He created us for far greater things.

Life's greatest rewards seldom fall into our laps; to the contrary, our greatest accomplishments usually require lots of work, which is perfectly fine with God. After all, He knows that we're up to the task, and He has big plans for us; may we, as disciplined believers, always be worthy of those plans.

☞ *Prudent, cautious self-control is wisdom's root.*

Robert Burns

☞ *Simply stated, self-discipline is obedience to God's Word and willingness to submit everything in life to His will, for His ultimate glory.*

John MacArthur

COMPASSIONATE SERVANTS

*Finally, all of you be of one mind, having compassion
for one another; love as brothers,
be tenderhearted, be courteous.*

1 Peter 3:8 NKJV

☞ God's Word commands us to be compassionate, generous servants to those who need our support. As believers, we have been richly blessed by our Creator. We, in turn, are called to share our gifts, our possessions, our testimonies, and our talents.

Concentration camp survivor Corrie ten Boom correctly observed, "The measure of a life is not its duration but its donation." These words remind us that the quality of our lives is determined not by what we are able to take from others, but instead by what we are able to share with others.

The thread of compassion is woven into the very fabric of Christ's teachings. If we are to be disciples of Christ, we, too, must be zealous in caring for others. Our Savior expects no less from us. And He deserves no less.

☞ *Compassion is sometimes the fatal capacity for feeling what it is like to live inside somebody else's skin. It is the knowledge that there can never really be any peace and joy for me until there is peace and joy finally for you too.*

Frederick Buechner

THE REMEDY FOR UNCERTAINTY

But He said to them, "Why are you fearful,
O you of little faith?" Then He arose and rebuked
the winds and the sea, and there was a great calm.

Matthew 8:26 NKJV

☞ In the 8th chapter of Matthew, we are told of a terrible storm that rose quickly on the Sea of Galilee while Jesus and His disciples were in a boat, far from shore. The disciples were filled with fear.

Sometimes, like Jesus' disciples, we feel threatened by the storms of life. Sometimes we may feel distant from God, and sometimes we may question His power or His plans. During these moments, when our hopes begin to fade and our fears begin to multiply, we must remember that God is not simply near, He is here.

Are you being tested? If so, remember that God is always with you, always willing to calm the storms of life. When you sincerely seek His presence—and when you genuinely seek to establish a deeper, more meaningful relationship with His Son—God is prepared to touch your heart, to calm your fears, to answer your doubts, and to restore your hopes.

☞ *Struggling with God over the issues of life doesn't show a lack of faith—that is faith.*

Lee Strobel

DISCOVERING GOD'S PLANS

*For it is God who works in you both to will
and to do for His good pleasure.*

Philippians 2:13 NKJV

☞ You can expect a satisfying and fulfilling life when
you follow God's plan for your life. But how can you
discern God's will? You should begin by studying
God's Word and obeying His commandments. You
should watch carefully for His signs, and you should
associate with fellow Christians who encourage your
spiritual growth. And you should listen to that inner
voice that speaks to you in the quiet moments of your
daily devotionals.

God intends to use you in wonderful, unexpected
ways if you let Him. The decision to seek God's
plan and to follow it is yours and yours alone. The
consequences of that decision have implications that
are both profound and eternal, so choose carefully.

☞ *Every man's life is a plan of God.*

Horace Bushnell

☞ *With God, it's never "Plan B" or "second best."
It's always "Plan A." And, if we let Him, He'll make
something beautiful of our lives.*

Gloria Gaither

BUILDING FELLOWSHIP

*Behold, how good and how pleasant it is
for brethren to dwell together in unity!*

Psalm 133:1 NKJV

☞ Every believer—including you—needs to be part of a community of faith. Your association with fellow Christians should be uplifting, enlightening, encouraging, and consistent.

Are you an active member of your fellowship? Are you a builder of bridges inside the four walls of your church and outside it? Do you contribute to God's glory by contributing your time and your talents to a close-knit band of hope-filled believers? Hopefully so. The fellowship of believers is intended to be a powerful tool for spreading God's Good News and uplifting His children. And God intends for you to be a fully contributing member of that fellowship. Your intentions should be the same.

☞ *One cannot arrive at and maintain individual conviction of faith in isolation from the already existing community of faith.*

Albrecht Ritschl

☞ *Be united with other Christians. A wall with loose bricks is not good. The bricks must be cemented together.*

Corrie ten Boom

Faith That Works

Thus also faith by itself,
if it does not have works, is dead.

James 2:17 NKJV

☞ Through every stage of your life, God stands by your side, ready to strengthen you and protect you . . . if you have faith in Him. When you place your faith, your trust, indeed your life in the hands of Christ Jesus, you'll be amazed at the marvelous things He can do with you and through you.

So make this promise to yourself and keep it: make certain that your faith is a faith that works. How? You can strengthen your faith through praise, through worship, through Bible study, and through prayer. When you do so, you'll learn to trust God's plans. With Him, all things are possible, and He stands ready to open a world of possibilities to you . . . if you have faith.

☞ *Faith is our spiritual oxygen. It not only keeps us alive in God, but enables us to grow stronger. . . .*

Joyce Landorf Heatherly

☞ *It is faith that saves us, not works, but the faith that saves us always produces works.*

C. H. Spurgeon

A WALK WITH GOD

For I have given you an example,
that you should do as I have done to you.

John 13:15 NKJV

☞ Jesus Christ is not only our Lord and Savior;
He is also the perfect example for how we should
live our lives. Every day, we are confronted with
countless opportunities to follow in the footsteps of
Jesus. When we do, our Heavenly Father guides our
steps and blesses our endeavors. As citizens of a fast-
changing world, we face challenges that sometimes
leave us feeling overworked, over-committed, and
overwhelmed. But God has different plans for us.
He intends that we slow down long enough to praise
Him and to glorify His Son. When we do, He lifts our
spirits and enriches our lives.

Today provides a glorious opportunity to place
yourself in the service of the One who is the Giver of
all blessings. May you seek His will, may you trust His
word, and may you walk in the footsteps of His Son.

☞ *The Christian faith is meant to be lived moment by*
moment. It isn't some broad, general outline—it's a long
walk with a real Person. Details count: passing thoughts,
small sacrifices, a few encouraging words, little acts of
kindness, brief victories over nagging sins.

Joni Eareckson Tada

ACCEPTING HIS ABUNDANCE

Give, and it will be given to you: good measure,
pressed down, shaken together, and running over will be
put into your bosom. For with the same measure that
you use, it will be measured back to you.

Luke 6:38 NKJV

☞ The Bible gives us hope—as Christians we can enjoy lives filled with abundance.

But what, exactly, did Jesus mean when, in John 10:10, He promised "life…more abundantly"? Was He referring to material possessions or financial wealth? Hardly. Jesus offers a different kind of abundance: a spiritual richness that extends beyond the temporal boundaries of this world.

Is material abundance part of God's plan for our lives? Perhaps. But in every circumstance of life, during times of wealth or times of want, God will provide us what we need if we trust Him (Matthew 6). May we, as believers, claim the riches of Christ Jesus every day that we live, and may we share His blessings with all who cross our path.

☞ *God has promised us abundance, peace, and eternal life. These treasures are ours for the asking; all we must do is claim them. One of the great mysteries of life is why on earth do so many of us wait so very long to lay claim to God's gifts?*

Marie T. Freeman

FORGIVENESS IS GOD'S WAY

Be kind and loving to each other, and forgive each other just as God forgave you in Christ.

Ephesians 4:32 NCV

☞ To forgive others is difficult. Being frail, fallible, imperfect human beings, we are quick to anger, quick to blame, slow to forgive, and even slower to forget. No matter. Forgiveness, no matter how difficult, is God's way, and it must be our way, too.

God's commandments are not intended to be customized for the particular whims of particular believers. God's word is not a menu from which each of us may select items à la carte, according to our own desires. Far from it. God's Holy Word is a book that must be taken in its entirety; all of God's commandments are to be taken seriously. And, so it is with forgiveness. So, if you hold bitterness against even a single person, forgive. Then, to the best of your abilities, forget. It's God's way for you to live.

☞ *Looking back over my life, all I can see is mercy and grace written in large letters everywhere. May God help me have the same kind of heart toward those who wound or offend me.*

Jim Cymbala

☞ *Forgiveness is rarely easy, but it is always right.*

Cynthia Heald

FRIENDS AND FAMILY

As iron sharpens iron, so people can improve each other.

Proverbs 27:17 NCV

☞ We can give thanks to our generous Heavenly Father for many things, but a loving family is a treasure from God, and so is a trustworthy friend. If you are a member of a close knit, supportive family, offer a word of thanks to your Creator. And if you have a close circle of trustworthy friends, consider yourself richly blessed.

Today, take time to praise God for your family and for your friends. God has placed these people along your path—love them and care for them. These people are, in a very real sense, gifts from God; we should treat them as such.

☞ *The best times in life are made a thousand times better when shared with a dear friend.*

Luci Swindoll

☞ *God often keeps us on the path by guiding us through the counsel of friends and trusted spiritual advisors.*

Bill Hybels

ACCEPTING YOURSELF

God began doing a good work in you,
and I am sure he will continue it until it is finished
when Jesus Christ comes again.

Philippians 1:6 NCV

☞ Accepting other people can be difficult. But sometimes, we find it even more difficult to accept ourselves.

We have high expectations and lofty goals. We want to achieve them now, not later. And, of course, we want our lives to unfold according to our own wishes and our own timetables—not God's.

The Bible affirms the importance of self-acceptance by exhorting believers to love others as they love themselves (Matthew 22:37-40). Furthermore, the Bible teaches that when we genuinely open our hearts to Him, God accepts us just as we are. And, if He accepts us—faults and all—then who are we to believe otherwise?

☞ *The great freedom Jesus gives us is to be ourselves, defined by His love and our inner qualities and gifts rather than by any kind of show we put on for the world.*

Leslie Williams

☞ *By the grace of God you are what you are; glory in your selfhood, accept yourself and go on from there.*

Wilferd Peterson

DECISION-MAKING 101

*Such doubters are thinking two different things at
the same time, and they cannot decide about
anything they do. They should not think they
will receive anything from the Lord.*

James 1:8 NCV

☞ Decisions! Decisions! Decisions! All day long you
must make decisions—decisions about the things you
do, decisions about the words you speak, and decisions
about the thoughts you choose to think.

If you're facing one of life's major decisions,
here are some things you can do: 1. Gather as much
information as you can. 2. Don't be too impulsive. 3.
Rely on the advice of trusted friends and mentors. 4.
Pray for guidance. 5. Trust the quiet inner voice of
your conscience 6. When the time for action arrives,
act. Procrastination is the enemy of progress; don't let
it defeat you.

People who can never quite seem to make up their
minds usually make themselves miserable. So when in
doubt, be decisive. It's the decent way to live.

☞ *There is no need to fear the decisions of life when you
know Jesus Christ, for His name is Counselor.*

Warren Wiersbe

☞ *No trumpets sound when the important decisions of
our life are made. Destiny is made known silently.*

Agnes DeMille

STRENGTH FOR THE DAY

I can do all things through Christ who strengthens me.

Philippians 4:13 NKJV

☞ Have you made God the cornerstone of your life, or is He relegated to a few hours on Sunday morning? Have you genuinely allowed God to reign over every corner of your heart, or have you attempted to place Him in a spiritual compartment? The answer to these questions will determine the direction of your day and your life.

God loves you. In times of trouble, He will comfort you; in times of sorrow, He will dry your tears. When you are or weak or sorrowful, God is as near as your next breath. He stands at the door of your heart and waits. Welcome Him in and allow Him to rule. And then, accept the peace, and the strength, and the protection, and the abundance that only God can give.

☞ *In my weakness, I have learned, like Moses, to lean hard on God. The weaker I am, the harder I lean on Him. The harder I lean, the stronger I discover Him to be. The stronger I discover God to be, the more resolute I am in this job He's given me to do.*

Joni Eareckson Tada

GOOD WORK

In all the work you are doing, work the best you can.
Work as if you were doing it for the Lord, not for people.

Colossians 3:23 NCV

☞ How does God intend for us to work? Does He intend for us to work diligently or does He, instead, reward mediocrity? The answer is obvious. God has created a world in which hard work is rewarded and sloppy work is not. Yet sometimes, we may seek ease over excellence, or we may be tempted to take shortcuts when God intends that we walk the straight and narrow path.

Today, heed God's Word by doing good work. Wherever you find yourself, whatever your job description, do your work, and do it with all your heart. When you do, you will most certainly win the recognition of your peers. But more importantly, God will bless your efforts and use you in ways that only He can understand. So do your work with focus and dedication. And leave the rest up to God.

☞ *I long to accomplish a great and noble task, but it is my chief duty to accomplish small tasks as if they were great and noble.*

Helen Keller

☞ *Think enthusiastically about everything, especially your work.*

Norman Vincent Peale

FILLED WITH THE SPIRIT

Do not be drunk with wine, which will ruin you,
but be filled with the Spirit.

Ephesians 5:18 NCV

☞ Are you burdened by the pressures of everyday living? If so, it's time to take the pressure off. How can you do so? By allowing the Holy Spirit to fill you and do His work in your life.

When you are filled with the Holy Spirit, your words and deeds will reflect a love and devotion to Christ. When you are filled with the Holy Sprit, the steps of your life's journey are guided by the Lord. When you allow God's Spirit to work in you and through you, you will be energized and transformed.

Today, allow yourself to be filled with the Spirit of God. And then stand back in amazement as God begins to work miracles in your own life and in the lives of those you love.

☞ *Whether we preach, pray, write, do business, travel, take care of children, or administer the government—whatever we do—our whole life and influence should be filled with the power of the Holy Spirit.*

Charles Finney

☞ *The Holy Spirit is like a living and continually flowing fountain in believers. We have the boundless privilege of tapping into that fountain every time we pray.*

Shirley Dobson

COMPASSIONATE CHRISTIANITY

*God has chosen you and made you his holy people.
He loves you. So always do these things: Show mercy
to others, be kind, humble, gentle, and patient.*

Colossians 3:12 NCV

☞ How can you practice compassionate Christianity?
By making kindness a centerpiece of your dealings
with others.

The instructions of Colossians 3:12 are unambiguous: as Christians, we are to be compassionate,
humble, gentle, and kind. But sometimes, we fall
short. In the busyness and confusion of daily life, we
may neglect to share a kind word or a kind deed. This
oversight hurts others, but it hurts us most of all.

Today, slow yourself down and be alert for those
who need your smile, your kind words, or your helping
hand. Today, honor Christ by following and obeying
His Golden Rule. He deserves no less, and neither, for
that matter, do your friends.

☞ *As much as God loves to hear our worship and
adoration, surely he delights all the more in seeing our
gratitude translated into simple kindnesses that keep the
chain of praise unbroken, alive in others' hearts.*

Evelyn Christenson

THE GREATEST OF THESE

And now abide faith, hope, love, these three;
but the greatest of these is love.

1 Corinthians 13:13 NKJV

☞ The beautiful words of 1st Corinthians 13 remind us that love is God's commandment: Faith is important, of course. So, too, is hope. But, love is more important still. We are commanded (not advised, not encouraged…commanded!) to love one another just as Christ loved us (John 13:34). That's a tall order, but as Christians, we are obligated to follow it.

Christ showed His love for us on the cross, and we are called upon to return Christ's love by sharing it. Today, let us spread Christ's love to families, friends, and even strangers, so that through us, others might come to know Him.

☞ *The cross symbolizes a cosmic as well as a historic truth. Love conquers the world, but its victory is not an easy one.*

Reinhold Neibuhr

☞ *There are only two duties required of us—the love of God and the love of our neighbor, and the surest sign of discovering whether we observe these duties is the love of our neighbor.*

St. Teresa of Avila

THE LOVE OF MONEY

For the love of money is a root of all kinds of evil,
for which some have strayed from the faith
in their greediness, and pierced themselves
through with many sorrows.

1 Timothy 6:10 NKJV

☞ Your money can be used as a blessing to yourself and to others, but beware: You live in a society that places far too much importance on money and the things that money can buy. God does not. God cares about people, not possessions, and so must you.

Money, in and of itself, is not evil; worshipping money is. So today, as you prioritize matters of importance for you and yours, remember that God is almighty, but the dollar is not.

If we worship God, we are blessed. But if we worship "the almighty dollar," we are inevitably punished because of our misplaced priorities—and our punishment inevitably comes sooner rather than later.

☞ *God is looking over the entire earth for men who have the proper attitude toward money and who will use it according to His direction and not according to their own interests.*

Larry Burkett

WHERE PEACE BEGINS

I leave you peace; my peace I give you.
I do not give it to you as the world does.
So don't let your hearts be troubled or afraid.

John 14:27 NCV

☞ Peace with God. Peace with self. Peace with others. Do you possess that kind of peace? Have you found the genuine peace that can be yours through Jesus Christ, or are you still rushing after the illusion of "peace and happiness" that the world promises but cannot deliver? The words of John 14:27 remind us that Jesus offers us peace, not as the world gives, but as He alone gives. Our challenge is to accept Christ's peace into our hearts and then, as best we can, to share His peace with our neighbors.

Today, as a gift to yourself, to your family, and to your friends, claim the inner peace that is your spiritual birthright: the peace of Jesus Christ. It is offered freely; it has been paid for in full; it is yours for the asking. So ask. And then share.

☞ *The better acquainted you become with God, the less tensions you feel and the more peace you possess.*

Charles Allen

☞ *Peace is full confidence that God is Who He says He is and that He will keep every promise in His Word.*

Dorothy Harrison Pentecost

GREAT HOPES, SENSIBLE RISKS

Is anything too hard for the Lord?

Genesis 18:14 NKJV

As we consider the uncertainties of the future, we are confronted with a powerful temptation: the temptation to "play it safe." Unwilling to move mountains, we fret over molehills. Unwilling to entertain great hopes for the tomorrow, we focus on the unfairness of the today. Unwilling to trust God completely, we take timid half-steps when God intends that we make giant leaps.

Today, ask God for the courage to step beyond the boundaries of your doubts. Ask Him to guide you to a place where you can realize your full potential—a place where you are freed from the fear of failure. Ask Him to do His part, and promise Him that you will do your part. Don't ask Him to lead you to a "safe" place; ask Him to lead you to the "right" place . . . and remember: those two places are seldom the same.

God is teaching me to become more and more "teachable": To keep evolving. To keep taking the risk of learning something new...or unlearning something old and off base.

Beth Moore

SHARING THE GOOD NEWS

*Christ did not send me to baptize people but to preach
the Good News. And he sent me to preach
the Good News without using words of human wisdom
so that the cross of Christ would not lose its power.*

1 Corinthians 1:17 NCV

☞ When sharing our testimonies, we, as Christians, must be courageous, forthright, and unashamed. In his second letter to Timothy, Paul offers a message to believers of every generation when he writes, "God did not give us a spirit that makes us afraid" (1:7 NCV).

We live in a world that desperately needs the healing message of Christ Jesus. Every believer, each in his or her own way, bears a personal responsibility for sharing that message. If you are a believer in Christ, you know how He has touched your heart and changed your life.

Now it's your turn to share the Good News with others. And remember: today is the perfect time to share your testimony because tomorrow may quite simply be too late.

☞ *Claim the joy that is yours. Pray. And know that your joy is used by God to reach others.*

Kay Arthur

SUFFICIENT FOR YOUR NEEDS

*And God is able to make all grace abound toward you,
that you, always having all sufficiency in all things,
may have an abundance for every good work.*

2 Corinthians 9:8 NKJV

✦ It is easy to become overwhelmed by the demands of everyday life, but if you're a faithful follower of the One from Galilee, you need never be overwhelmed. Why? Because God's love is sufficient to meet your needs. Whatever dangers you may face, whatever heartbreaks you must endure, God is with you, and He stands ready to comfort you and to heal you.

The Psalmist writes, "Weeping may endure for a night, but joy comes in the morning" (Psalm 30:5 NKJV). But when we are suffering, the morning may seem very far away. It is not. God promises that He is "near to those who have a broken heart" (Psalm 34:18 NKJV).

If you are experiencing the intense pain of a recent loss, or if you are still mourning a loss from long ago, perhaps you are now ready to begin the next stage of your journey with God. If so, be mindful of this fact: the loving heart of God is sufficient to meet any challenge, including yours.

✦ *The grace of God is sufficient for all our needs.*

Peter Marshall

THE PROMISE OF STRENGTH

*But may the God of all grace, who called us to
His eternal glory by Christ Jesus, after you have suffered
a while, perfect, establish, strengthen, and settle you.*

1 Peter 5:10 NKJV

✦ God promises us eternal life through His Son Jesus
Christ, but God does not promise us that our earthly
lives will be free from suffering. Instead, He promises
that He will give comfort to the suffering, strength
to the weary and healing to those who grieve. God
promises that wherever we are, whether at the peak
of the mountaintop or in the darkness of the deepest
valley, He will be with us always . . . and that promise,
dear friends, is always enough.

✦ *Part of every misery is, so to speak, the misery's shadow
or reflection: the fact that you don't merely suffer but
that you have to keep on thinking about the fact that you
suffer. I not only live each endless day in grief, but I live
each day thinking about living each day in grief.*

C. S. Lewis

✦ *The love of God exists in its strongest and purest form
in the very midst of suffering and tragedy.*

Suzanne Dale Ezell

EXCELLENCE, NOT EXCUSES

Do you see people skilled in their work?
They will work for kings, not for ordinary people.

Proverbs 22:29 NCV

❧ President Harry Truman kept a sign on his desk that read, "The Buck Stops Here." In a sense, that sign applies to each of us. If we wish to become capable adults, we must take responsibility for our actions, and we must resist the temptation to make excuses for our failures.

Excuses are everywhere . . . excellence is not. If you seek excellence (and the rewards that accompany it), you must carefully refrain from the habit of excuse making.

Whatever your job description, it's up to you, and no one else, to become a master of your craft. It's up to you to do your job right—and to do it right now. Wherever you happen to be, the buck stops there, and it's up to you not to pass it.

❧ *We need to stop focusing on our lacks and stop giving out excuses and start looking at and listening to Jesus.*

Anne Graham Lotz

❧ *Few things fire up a person's commitment like dedication to excellence.*

John Maxwell

FAITH VERSUS FEAR

Don't be afraid, because I am your God.
I will make you strong and will help you;
I will support you with my right hand that saves you.

Isaiah 41:10 NCV

✦ Although God has guided us through our struggles and troubles many times before, it is easy for us to lose hope whenever we face adversity, uncertainty, or unwelcome changes.

The next time you find yourself facing a fear-provoking situation, remember that the One who calmed the wind and the waves is also your personal Savior. Then ask yourself which is stronger: your faith or your fear. The answer should be obvious. So, when the storm clouds form overhead and you find yourself being tossed on the stormy seas of life, remember this: Wherever you are, God is there, too. And, because He cares for you, you are protected.

✦ *His hand on me is a father's hand, gently guiding and encouraging. His hand lets me know he is with me, so I am not afraid.*

Mary Morrison Suggs

✦ *Courage faces fear and thereby masters it. Cowardice represses fear and is thereby mastered by it.*

Martin Luther King, Jr.

The Courage to Live Boldly

For God has not given us a spirit of fear,
but of power and of love and of a sound mind.

2 Timothy 1:7 NKJV

✦ You cannot fix what you will not face. So here's a question that's worth asking yourself: Do you prefer to face your fears or run from them? The answer to this question will determine the direction and quality of your life.

When Paul wrote Timothy, he reminded his young protégé that the God they served was a bold God, and God's spirit empowered His children with boldness also. Like Timothy, we face times of uncertainty and fear. God's message is the same to us, today, as it was to Timothy: We can live boldly because the spirit of God resides in us.

So today, as you face the challenges of everyday living, remember that God is with you . . . and you are protected.

✦ *The Holy Spirit is no skeptic, and the things he has written in our hearts are not doubts or opinions, but assertions—surer and more certain than sense or life itself.*

Martin Luther

BELIEVING MAKES A DIFFERENCE

You have not seen Christ, but still you love him.
You cannot see him now, but you believe in him.
So you are filled with a joy that cannot be explained,
a joy full of glory. And you are receiving the goal of
your faith—the salvation of your souls.

1 Peter 1:8-9 NCV

✦ Do you weave your beliefs into the very fabric of your day? If you do, God will honor your good works, and your good works will honor God.

If you seek to be a responsible believer, you must realize that it is never enough to hear the instructions of God; you must also live by them. And it is never enough to wait idly by while others to do God's work here on earth. You, too, must act.

Doing God's work is a responsibility that every Christian (including you) should bear. And when you do, your loving Heavenly Father will reward your efforts with a bountiful harvest.

✦ *If all things are possible with God, then all things are possible to him who believes in him.*

Corrie ten Boom

✦ *Faith is to believe what you do not see; the reward of this faith is to see what you believe.*

St. Augustine

Too Busy

The plans of hard-working people earn a profit,
but those who act too quickly become poor.

Proverbs 21:5 NCV

✦ Are you one of those believers who is simply too busy for their own good? Has the hectic pace of life robbed you of the peace that might otherwise be yours through Jesus Christ? If so, you're doing a disservice to yourself and your family.

Through His Son Jesus, God offers you a peace that passes human understanding, but He won't force His peace upon you; in order to experience it, you must slow down long enough to sense His presence and His love.

Today, as a gift to yourself, to your family, and to the world, be still and claim the inner peace that is your spiritual birthright—the peace of Jesus Christ. It is offered freely; it has been paid for in full; it is yours for the asking. So ask. And then share.

✦ *It's ironic that one of the best remedies for impending burnout is to give yourself away—to pick out one time and place each week where you can stretch out your hands for the pure joy of doing it.*

Liz Curtis Higgs

✦ *We often become mentally and spiritually barren because we're so busy.*

Franklin Graham

HOW WE THANK HIM

*We always thank God, the Father of our
Lord Jesus Christ.*

Colossians 1:3 NCV

✦ How do we thank God for the gifts He has given us?
By using those gifts for the glory of His kingdom.

God has given you talents and opportunities that
are uniquely yours. Are you willing to use your gifts
in the way that God intends? And are you willing to
summon the discipline that is required develop your
talents and to hone your skills? That's precisely what
God wants you to do, and that's precisely what you
should desire for yourself.

As you seek to expand your talents, you will
undoubtedly encounter stumbling blocks along the
way, such as the fear of rejection or the fear of failure.
When you do, don't stumble! Just continue to refine
your skills, and offer your services to God. And when
the time is right, He will use you—but it's up to you
to be thoroughly prepared when He does.

✦ *One thing taught large in the Holy Scriptures is that
while God gives His gifts freely, He will require a strict
accounting of them at the end of the road. Each man is
personally responsible for his store, be it large or small,
and will be required to explain his use of it before the
judgment seat of Christ.*

A. W. Tozer

INFINITE LOVE

*For I am persuaded that neither death nor life,
nor angels nor principalities nor powers, nor things
present nor things to come, nor height nor depth, nor any
other created thing, shall be able to separate us from
the love of God which is in Christ Jesus our Lord.*

Romans 8:38-39 NKJV

✦ Christ's love for you is both intimate and personal. He gave His life so that you might have the gift of eternal life. His love is unbounded by time or circumstance.

Are you willing to experience an intimate relationship with Jesus? Your Savior is waiting patiently; don't make Him wait a single minute longer. Embrace His love today.

✦ *Christ is like a river that is continually flowing. There are always fresh supplies of water coming from the fountainhead, so that a man may live by it and be supplied with water all his life. So Christ is an ever-flowing fountain; he is continually supplying his people, and the fountain is not spent. They who live upon Christ may have fresh supplies from him for all eternity; they may have an increase of blessedness that is new, and new still, and which never will come to an end.*

Jonathan Edwards

NO COMPLAINTS

Do everything without complaining or arguing.
Then you will be innocent and without any wrong.

Philippians 2:14-15 NCV

✦ It is strange but true—all too often, we allow a few negative experiences to dominate our thoughts and, by extension, our lives. Why? Because we are imperfect human beings who often lose sight of our blessings. Ironically, most of us have more blessings than we can count, but we may still find reasons to complain about the minor frustrations of everyday life. To do so, of course, is not only wrong; it is also the pinnacle of shortsightedness and a serious roadblock on the path to spiritual abundance.

Are you tempted to complain about the inevitable minor frustrations of everyday living? Don't do it! Today and every day, make it a practice to count your blessings, not your hardships.

✦ *Thanksgiving or complaining—these words express two contrastive attitudes of the souls of God's children in regard to His dealings with them. The soul that gives thanks can find comfort in everything; the soul that complains can find comfort in nothing.*

Hannah Whitall Smith

THE MORNING WATCH

Every morning he wakes me. He teaches me to listen
like a student. The Lord God helps me learn…

Isaiah 50:4-5 NCV

✦ Each new day is a gift from God, and if you are wise, you will spend a few quiet moments each morning thanking the Giver.

Warren Wiersbe writes, "Surrender your mind to the Lord at the beginning of each day." And that's sound advice. When you begin each day with your head bowed and your heart lifted, you are reminded of God's love, His protection, and His commandments. Then, you can align your priorities for the coming day with the teachings and commandments that God has placed upon your heart.

So, if you've acquired the unfortunate habit of trying to "squeeze" God into the corners of your life, it's time to reshuffle the items on your to-do list by placing God first. And if you haven't already done so, form the habit of spending quality time with your Father in heaven. He deserves it . . . and so do you.

✦ *Think of this—we may live together with Him here and now, a daily walking with Him who loved us and gave Himself for us.*

Elisabeth Elliot

DURING DARK DAYS

I have heard your prayer, I have seen your tears;
surely I will heal you.

2 Kings 20:5 NKJV

✤ The sadness that accompanies any significant loss is an inevitable fact of life. In time, sadness runs its course and gradually abates. Depression, on the other hand, is a physical and emotional condition that is highly treatable.

If you find yourself feeling "blue," perhaps it's a logical reaction to the ups and downs of daily life. But if you or someone close to you have become dangerously depressed, it's time to seek a professional evaluation.

Some days are light and happy, and some days are not. When we face the inevitable dark days of life, we must choose how we will respond. Will we allow ourselves to sink even more deeply into our own sadness, or will we do the difficult work of pulling ourselves out? We bring light to the dark days of life by turning first to God, and then to trusted family members, friends, and health professionals. When we do, the clouds will eventually part, and the sun will shine once more upon our souls.

✤ *What the devil loves is that vague cloud of unspecified guilt feeling or unspecified virtue by which he lures us into despair.*

C. S. Lewis

THE POWER OF ENCOURAGING WORDS

When you talk, do not say harmful things,
but say what people need—words that will help others
become stronger. Then what you say will do good
to those who listen to you.

Ephesians 4:29 NCV

✤ God's Word is filled with illustrations and admonitions concerning the power of the words we speak. Our words have the power to do great good or great harm. If we offer words of encouragement and hope, we can lift others up. And that's precisely what God commands us to do.

Sometimes, when we feel uplifted and secure, it is easy to speak kind words. Other times, when we are discouraged or tired, we can scarcely summon the energy to uplift ourselves, much less anyone else. God intends that we speak words of kindness, wisdom, and truth, no matter our circumstances, no matter our emotions. When we do, we share a priceless gift with the world, and we give glory to the One who gave His life for us. As believers, we must do no less.

✤ *The truest help we can render an afflicted man is not to take his burden from him, but to call out his best energy, that he may be able to bear the burden himself.*

Phillips Brooks

GOD'S LESSONS

The Lord says, "I will make you wise and show you
where to go. I will guide you and watch over you."

Psalms 32:8 NCV

✦ When it comes to learning life's lessons, we can either do things the easy way or the hard way. The easy way can be summed up as follows: when God teaches us a lesson, we learn it . . . the first time! Unfortunately, too many of us learn much more slowly than that.

When we resist God's instruction, He continues to teach us, whether we like it or not. Our challenge, then, is to discern God's lessons from the experiences of everyday life. Hopefully, we learn those lessons sooner rather than later because the sooner we do, the sooner He can move on to the next lesson and the next, and the next . . .

✦ *True learning can take place at every age of life, and it doesn't have to be in the curriculum plan.*

Suzanne Dale Ezell

✦ *The wise man gives proper appreciation in his life to this past. He learns to sift the sawdust of heritage in order to find the nuggets that make the current moment have any meaning.*

Grady Nutt

FAITH THAT MOVES MOUNTAINS

*I tell you the truth, you can say to this mountain,
"Go, fall into the sea." And if you have no doubts in
your mind and believe that what you say will happen,
God will do it for you.*

Mark 11:23 NCV

✦ Because we live in a demanding world, all of us have mountains to climb and mountains to move. Moving those mountains requires faith.

Are you a mountain mover whose faith is evident for all to see? Hopefully so. God needs more men and women who are willing to move mountains for His glory and for His kingdom.

God walks with you, ready and willing to strengthen you. Accept His strength today. And remember—Jesus taught His disciples that if they had faith, they could move mountains. You can too . . . so with no further ado, let the mountain-moving begin.

✦ *Only God can move mountains, but faith and prayer can move God.*

E. M. Bounds

✦ *God never calls without enabling us. In other words, if he calls you to do something, he makes it possible for you to do it.*

Luci Swindoll

In God We Trust

*And my God shall supply all your need according to
His riches in glory by Christ Jesus.*

Philippians 4:19 NKJV

✦ Countless books have been written about money—
how to make it and how to keep it. But if you're a
Christian, you probably already own at least one
copy—and probably several copies—of the world's
foremost guide to financial security. That book is
the Holy Bible. God's Word is not only a roadmap to
eternal life, it is also an indispensable guidebook for
life here on earth. As such, the Bible has much to say
about your life, your faith, and your finances.

If you're in need of a financial makeover, God's
Word can help. In fact, Biblical principles can help
you organize your financial life in such a way that you
have less need to worry and more time to celebrate
God's glorious creation. If that sounds appealing,
open your Bible, read its instructions, and follow
them.

✦ *Here's a good recipe for managing your money: Never
make a big financial decision without first talking it over
with God.*

Marie T. Freeman

LOVE THAT FORGIVES

*And whenever you stand praying, if you have anything
against anyone, forgive him, that your Father in heaven
may also forgive you your trespasses.*

Mark 11:25 NKJV

✦ Genuine love is an exercise in forgiveness. If we
wish to build lasting relationships, we must learn
how to forgive. Why? Because our loved ones are
imperfect (as are we). How often must we forgive our
family and friends? More times than we can count.
Why? Because that's what God wants us to do.

Perhaps granting forgiveness is hard for you. If
so, you are not alone. Genuine, lasting forgiveness
is often difficult to achieve—difficult but not
impossible. Thankfully, with God's help, all things
are possible, and that includes forgiveness. But, even
though God is willing to help, He expects you to do
some of the work. And make no mistake: forgiveness
is work, which is okay with God. He knows that the
payoffs are worth the effort.

✦ *We pardon to the degree that we love.*

François de la Rochefoucauld

✦ *God expects us to forgive others as He has forgiven us;
we are to follow His example by having a forgiving heart.*

Vonette Bright

THE SEEDS OF GENEROSITY

Freely you have received, freely give.

Matthew 10:8 NKJV

❖ When we sow the seeds of generosity, we reap bountiful rewards in accordance with God's plan for our lives. Thus, we are instructed to give cheerfully and without reservation: "But this I say: He who sows sparingly will also reap sparingly, and he who sows bountifully will also reap bountifully. So let each one give as he purposes in his heart, not grudgingly or of necessity; for God loves a cheerful giver" (2 Corinthians 9:6-7 NKJV).

Today, make this pledge and keep it: Be a cheerful, generous, courageous giver. The world needs your help, and you need the spiritual rewards that will be yours when you give it.

❖ *All the blessings we enjoy are divine deposits, committed to our trust on this condition: that they should be dispensed for the benefit of our neighbors.*

John Calvin

❖ *When somebody needs a helping hand, he doesn't need it tomorrow or the next day. He needs it now, and that's exactly when you should offer to help. Good deeds, if they are really good, happen sooner rather than later.*

Marie T. Freeman

HIS TRANSFORMING POWER

Your old sinful self has died,
and your new life is kept with Christ in God.

Colossians 3:3 NCV

✦ Righteous believers who fashion their days around Jesus see the world differently; they act differently, and they feel differently about themselves and their neighbors. Hopefully, you, too, will be such a believer. God's hand has the power to transform your day and your life. Your task is to accept Christ's grace with a humble, thankful heart as you receive the "new life" that can be yours through Him.

Do you desire to improve some aspect of your life? If so, don't expect changing circumstances to miraculously transform you into the person you want to become. Transformation starts with God, and it starts in the quiet corners of a willing human heart—like yours.

✦ *God's work is not in buildings, but in transformed lives.*

Ruth Bell Graham

✦ *God's omniscience can instill you with a supernatural confidence that can transform your life.*

Bill Hybels

HE REIGNS

In all your ways acknowledge Him,
and He shall direct your paths.

Proverbs 3:6 NKJV

❖ Your Heavenly Father may not always reveal Himself as quickly (or as clearly) as you would like. But rest assured: God is in control, God is here, and God intends to use you in wonderful, unexpected ways.

God is sovereign. He reigns over the entire universe and He reigns over your little corner of that universe. Your challenge is to recognize God's sovereignty and live in accordance with His commandments. Sometimes, of course, this is easier said than done.

God desires to lead you along a path of His choosing. Your challenge is to watch, to listen, to learn . . . and to follow.

❖ *As you place yourself under the sovereign lordship of Jesus Christ, each mistake or failure can lead you right back to the throne.*

Barbara Johnson

❖ *Depositing our faith in Jesus Christ means God is now responsible for us, because He has purchased us.*

Franklin Graham

There's Work to Do

*The one who plants and the one who waters have
the same purpose, and each will be rewarded
for his own work.*

1 Corinthians 3:8 NCV

✦ God has work for you to do, but He won't make
you do it. Since the days of Adam and Eve, God has
allowed His children to make choices for themselves,
and so it is with you. You've got choices to make . . .
lots of them. If you choose wisely, you'll be rewarded;
if you choose unwisely, you'll bear the consequences.

Whether you're in school, at home, or in the
workplace, your success will depend, in large part,
upon the quality and quantity of your work. God has
created a world in which diligence is rewarded and
sloth is not. So whatever you choose to do, do it with
commitment, excitement, and vigor.

God did not create you for a life of mediocrity; He
created you for far greater things. Reaching for greater
things usually requires work and lots of it, which is
perfectly fine with God. After all, He knows that
you're up to the task, and He has big plans for you.
Very big plans...

✦ *We must trust as if it all depended on God and work as
if it all depended on us.*

C. H. Spurgeon

HEALTHY CHOICES

Why are you cast down, O my soul? And why are you disquieted within me? Hope in God; For I shall yet praise Him, The help of my countenance and my God.

Psalm 42:11 NKJV

✦ The journey toward improved health is not only a common-sense exercise in personal discipline, it is also a spiritual journey ordained by our Creator. God does not intend that we abuse our bodies by giving in to excessive appetites or to slothful behavior. To the contrary, God has instructed us to protect our physical bodies to the greatest extent we can. To do otherwise is to disobey Him.

God's plan for you includes provisions for your spiritual, physical, and emotional health. But, He expects you to do your fair share of the work! In a world that is chock-full of tasty temptations, you may find it all too easy to make unhealthy choices. Your challenge, of course, is to resist those unhealthy temptations by every means you can, including prayer. And rest assured: when you ask for God's help, He will give it.

✦ *People are funny. When they are young, they will spend their health to get wealth. Later, they will gladly pay all they have trying to get their health back.*

John Maxwell

FINDING HOPE

*These things I have spoken to you, that in Me you may
have peace. In the world you will have tribulation;
but be of good cheer, I have overcome the world.*

John 16:33 NKJV

✦ There are few sadder sights on earth than the sight of a person who has lost all hope. In difficult times, hope can be elusive, but Christians need never lose it. After all, God is good; His love endures; He has promised His children the gift of eternal life.

If you find yourself falling into the spiritual traps of worry and discouragement, consider the words of Jesus. It was Christ who promised, "In the world you will have tribulation; but be of good cheer, I have overcome the world." This world is indeed a place of trials and tribulations, but as believers, we are secure. God has promised us peace, joy, and eternal life. And, of course, God always keeps His promises.

✦ *And still today, when you boil it all down, our message to the world—even to the world that comes disguised as our child's schoolteacher, our next-door neighbor, or our personal hair stylist—is hope. Hope beyond the slavery of sin. And hope beyond the grave.*

Becky Tirabassi

A POSITIVE INFLUENCE

*Be an example to the believers in word, in conduct,
in love, in spirit, in faith, in purity.*

1 Timothy 4:12 NKJV

✦ As followers of Christ, we must each ask ourselves
an important question: "What kind of example am I?"
The answer to that question determines, in large part,
whether or not we are positive influences on our own
little corners of the world.

Phillips Brooks advised, "Be such a man, and
live such a life, that if every man were such as you,
and every life a life like yours, this earth would be
God's Paradise." And that's sound advice for men
and women alike because our families and friends are
watching . . . and so, for that matter, is God.

✦ *If you want your neighbor to know what Christ will
do for him, let the neighbor see what Christ has done for
you.*

Henry Ward Beecher

✦ *Let us preach you, Dear Jesus, without preaching, not
by words but by our example, by the casting force, the
sympathetic influence of what we do, the evident fullness
of the love our hearts bear to you. Amen.*

Mother Teresa

THE MIRACLE WORKER

Depend on the Lord and his strength;
always go to him for help. Remember the miracles
he has done; remember his wonders and his decisions.

Psalm 105:4-5 NCV

✦ If you haven't seen any of God's miracles lately, you haven't been looking. Throughout history, the Creator has intervened in the course of human events in ways that cannot be explained by science or human rationale. And He's still doing so today.

God's miracles are not limited to special occasions, nor are they witnessed by a select few. God is crafting His wonders all around us: the miracle of the birth of a new baby; the miracle of a world renewing itself with every sunrise; the miracle of lives transformed by God's love and grace. Each day, God's handiwork is evident for all to see and experience.

Today, seize the opportunity to inspect God's hand at work. His miracles come in a variety of shapes and sizes, so keep your eyes and your heart open. Be watchful, and you'll soon be amazed.

✦ *I believe that God is in the miracle business—that his favorite way of working is to pick up where our human abilities and understandings leave off and then do something so wondrous and unexpected that there's no doubt who the God is around here.*

Emilie Barnes

GOD'S GUIDANCE AND YOUR PATH

*Trust in the Lord with all your heart, and lean not
on your own understanding; in all your ways
acknowledge Him, and He shall direct your paths.*

Proverbs 3:5-6 NKJV

✦ Proverbs 3:5-6 makes this promise: if you
acknowledge God's sovereignty over every aspect of
your life, He will guide your path. And when you
walk along the path that God has created for you,
you'll experience a sense of purpose, a passion for
living, and a sense of peace that would otherwise
have eluded you.

As you prayerfully consider the direction that God
intends for you to take, here are things you should do:
You should study His Word and be watchful for His
signs. You should associate with fellow believers who
will encourage your spiritual growth. You should listen
carefully to that inner voice that speaks to you in the
quiet moments of your daily devotionals. When you
listen, God will speak . . . and the rest is up to you.

✦ *God's riches are beyond anything we could ask or even
dare to imagine! If my life gets gooey and stale, I have no
excuse.*

Barbara Johnson

CONDUCT AND CHARACTER

*Lead a quiet and peaceable life in all godliness
and reverence.*

1 Timothy 2:2 NKJV

✦ As believers in Christ, we must seek to live each day with discipline, honesty, and faith. When we do, at least two things happen: integrity becomes a habit, and God blesses us because of our obedience to Him.

Living a life of integrity isn't always the easiest way, but it is always the right way . . . and God clearly intends that it should be our way, too. Charles Stanley said, "The Bible teaches that we are accountable to one another for our conduct and character."

Character is forged on the anvil of honorable work and polished by the twin virtues of honesty and fairness. Character is a precious thing—difficult to build and wonderful to behold.

✦ *Often, our character is at greater risk in prosperity than in adversity.*

Beth Moore

✦ *What lessons about honor did you learn from your childhood? Are you living what you learned today?*

Dennis Swanberg

PRAISE HIM

Praise the Lord! Oh, give thanks to the Lord,
for He is good! For His mercy endures forever.

Psalm 106:1 NKJV

✦ God has blessed us immeasurably and we owe Him our everlasting praise. Yet Sometimes, in our rush "to get things done," we simply don't stop long enough to pause and thank our Creator for the countless blessings He has bestowed upon us.

When we slow down and express our gratitude to the One who made us, we enrich our own lives and the lives of those around us. Thus thanksgiving should become a habit, a regular part of our daily routines. God has blessed us beyond measure, and we owe Him everything, including our never-ending praise. Let us praise Him today, tomorrow, and throughout eternity.

✦ *Maintaining a focus on God will take our praise to heights that nothing else can.*

Jeff Walling

✦ *Praise Him! Praise Him! Tell of His excellent greatness. Praise Him! Praise Him! Ever in joyful song!*

Fanny Crosby

THE POWER OF WORDS

The wise don't tell everything they know,
but the foolish talk too much and are ruined.

Proverbs 10:14 NCV

❧ All too often, in the rush to have ourselves heard, we speak first and think next…with unfortunate results. God's Word reminds us that, "Careless words stab like a sword, but wise words bring healing" (Proverbs 12: 18 NCV). If we seek to be a source of encouragement to friends and family, then we must measure our words carefully. Words are important: they can hurt or heal. Words can uplift us or discourage us, and reckless words, spoken in haste, cannot be erased.

Today, measure your words carefully. Use words of kindness and praise, not words of anger or derision. Remember that you have the power to heal others or to injure them, to lift others up or to hold them back. When you lift them up, your wisdom will bring healing and comfort to a world that needs both.

❧ *The battle of the tongue is won not in the mouth, but in the heart.*

Annie Chapman

❧ *In all your deeds and words, you should look on Jesus as your model, whether you are keeping silence or speaking, whether you are alone or with others.*

St. Bonaventure

A QUIET PLACE

Now in the morning, having risen a long while
before daylight, He went out and departed
to a solitary place; and there He prayed.

Mark 1:35 NKJV

◈ In the first chapter of Mark, we read that in the darkness of the early morning hours, Jesus went to a solitary place and prayed. So, too, should we. But sometimes, finding quiet moments of solitude is difficult indeed. We live in a noisy world, a world filled with distractions, frustrations, and complications. But if we allow the distractions of a clamorous world to separate us from God's peace, we do ourselves a profound disservice. Are you one of those busy people who rush through the day with scarcely a single moment for quiet contemplation and prayer? If so, it's time to reorder your priorities. Nothing is more important than the time you spend with your Savior. So be still and claim the inner peace that is your spiritual birthright: the peace of Jesus Christ.

◈ *We Christians must simplify our lives or lose untold treasures on earth and in eternity. Modern civilization is so complex as to make the devotional life all but impossible. The need for solitude and quietness was never greater than it is today.*

A. W. Tozer

No Shortcuts

*But thanks be to God, who gives us the victory through
our Lord Jesus Christ. Therefore, my beloved brethren,
be steadfast, immovable, always abounding in
the work of the Lord, knowing that your labor
is not in vain in the Lord.*

1 Corinthians 15:57-58 NKJV

⇥ The world often tempts us with instant gratification:
get rich—today; lose weight—today; have everything
you want—today. Yet life's experiences and God's
Word tell us that the best things in life require
heaping helpings of both time and work.

It has been said, quite correctly, that there are no
shortcuts to any place worth going. For believers, it's
important to remember that hard work is not simply
a proven way to get ahead, it's also part of God's plan
for His children.

So do yourself this favor: don't look for shortcuts
. . . because there aren't any.

⇥ *It may be that the day of judgment will dawn tomorrow;
in that case, we shall gladly stop working for a better
tomorrow. But not before.*

Dietrich Bonhoeffer

⇥ *Ordinary work, which is what most of us do most of
the time, is ordained by God every bit as much as is the
extraordinary.*

Elisabeth Elliot

A WALK WITH GOD

Come to Me, all you who labor and are heavy laden,
and I will give you rest. Take My yoke upon you
and learn from Me, for I am gentle and lowly in heart,
and you will find rest for your souls.
For My yoke is easy and My burden is light.

Matthew 11:28-30 NKJV

❧ Are you tired? Discouraged? Fearful? Be comforted. Take a walk with God. Jesus called upon believers to walk with Him, and He promised them that He would teach them how to live freely and lightly (Matthew 11:28-30). Are you worried or anxious? Be confident in God's power. He will never desert you. Do you see no hope for the future? Be courageous and call upon God. He will protect you and then use you according to His purposes. Are you grieving? Know that God hears your suffering. He will comfort you and, in time, He will dry your tears. Are you confused? Listen to the quiet voice of your Heavenly Father. He is not a God of confusion. Talk with Him; listen to Him; follow His commandments. He is steadfast, and He is your Protector...forever.

❧ As a child of God, rest in the knowledge that your Savior precedes you, and He will walk with you through each experience of your life.

Henry Blackaby

CHOOSING THE GOOD LIFE

And in that day you will ask Me nothing.
Most assuredly, I say to you, whatever you ask
the Father in My name He will give you.
Until now you have asked nothing in My name.
Ask, and you will receive, that your joy may be full.

John 16:23-24 NKJV

◈ God offers us abundance through His Son, Jesus. Whether or not we accept God's abundance is, of course, up to each of us. When we entrust our hearts and our days to the One who created us, we experience abundance through the grace and sacrifice of His Son, Jesus. But, when we turn our thoughts and our energies away from God's commandments, we inevitably forfeit the spiritual abundance that might otherwise be ours.

What is your focus today? Are you focused on God's Word and His will for your life? Or are you focused on the distractions and temptations of a difficult world? If you sincerely seek the spiritual abundance that your Savior offers, then follow Him completely and without reservation. When you do, you will receive the love, the life, and the abundance that He has promised.

◈ *The gift of God is eternal life, spiritual life, abundant life through faith in Jesus Christ, the Living Word of God.*

Anne Graham Lotz

BEYOND ADDICTION

*Therefore submit to God. Resist the devil and he will
flee from you. Draw near to God and He will draw near
to you. Cleanse your hands, you sinners;
and purify your hearts, you double-minded.*

James 4:7-8 NKJV

⊰ Unless you're living on a deserted island, you
know people who are full-blown addicts—probably
lots of people. The dictionary defines addiction as
"the compulsive need for a habit-forming substance;
the condition of being habitually and compulsively
occupied with something." That definition is
accurate, but incomplete. For Christians, addiction
has an additional meaning: it means compulsively
worshipping something other than God.

If you, or someone you love, is suffering from the
blight of addiction, remember this: Help is available.
And if you're one of those fortunate people who
has never experimented with addictive substances,
congratulations. You have just have spared yourself a
lifetime of headaches and heartaches.

⊰ *We are meant to be addicted to God, but we develop
secondary additions that temporarily appear to fix our
problems.*

Edward M. Berckman

THE WISDOM TO CELEBRATE

A happy heart is like a continual feast.

Proverbs 15:15 NCV

❧ What will be your attitude today? Will you be fearful, angry, bored, or worried? Will you be cynical, bitter or pessimistic? If so, God wants to have a little talk with you.

The Christian life is a cause for celebration, but sometimes we don't feel much like celebrating. In fact, when the weight of the world seems to bear down upon our shoulders, celebration may be the last thing on our minds . . . but it shouldn't be. As God's children, we are all blessed beyond measure on good days and bad. This day is a non-renewable resource—once it's gone, it's gone forever.

God created you in His own image, and He wants you to experience hope and abundance. So today, and every day thereafter, celebrate the life that God has given you. Give thanks to the One who has given you everything, and trust in your heart that He wants to give you so much more.

❧ *You've heard the saying, 'Life is what you make it.' That means we have a choice. We can choose to have a life full of frustration and fear, but we can just as easily choose one of joy and contentment.*

Dennis Swanberg

A BOOK UNLIKE ANY OTHER

For I am not ashamed of the gospel of Christ, for it is the power of God to salvation for everyone who believes.

Romans 1:16 NKJV

◁ The Bible is a priceless gift, a tool for Christians to use as they share the Good News of their Savior, Christ Jesus. Too many Christians, however, keep their spiritual tool kits tightly closed and out of sight, with predictably unfortunate results.

God's Word is unlike any other book. A. W. Tozer wrote, "The purpose of the Bible is to bring men to Christ, to make them holy and prepare them for heaven. In this it is unique among books, and it always fulfills its purpose."

George Mueller observed, "The vigor of our spiritual lives will be in exact proportion to the place held by the Bible in our lives and in our thoughts." As Christians, we are called upon to study God's Holy Word and then to share it with the world.

God's Holy Word is, indeed, a priceless, one-of-a-kind treasure. Handle it with care, but, more importantly, handle it every day.

◁ *Unless we form the habit of going to the Bible in bright moments as well as in trouble, we cannot fully respond to its consolations because we lack equilibrium between light and darkness.*

Helen Keller

THIS IS HIS DAY

*This is the day the LORD has made;
we will rejoice and be glad in it.*

Psalm 118:24 *NKJV*

⋑ The 118th Psalm reminds us that today, like every other day, is a cause for celebration. God gives us this day; He fills it to the brim with possibilities, and He challenges us to use it for His purposes. The day is presented to us fresh and clean at midnight, free of charge, but we must beware: Today is a non-renewable resource—once it's gone, it's gone forever. Our responsibility, of course, is to use this day in the service of God's will and according to His commandments.

Today, treasure the time that God has given you. Give Him the glory and the praise and the thanksgiving that He deserves. And search for the hidden possibilities that God has placed along your path. This day is a priceless gift from God, so use it joyfully and encourage others to do likewise. After all, this is the day the Lord has made….

⋑ *All our life is a celebration for us; we are convinced, in fact, that God is always everywhere. We sing while we work…we pray while we carry out all life's other occupations.*

St. Clement of Alexandria

His Intimate Love

As the Father loved Me, I also have loved you;
abide in My love.

John 15:9 NKJV

⌁ Billy Graham observed, "God loves you and wants you to experience peace and life—abundant and eternal." Do you believe those words? Do you seek an intimate, one-on-one relationship with your Heavenly Father, or are you satisfied to keep Him at a "safe" distance?

Sometimes, in the crush of our daily duties, God may seem far away, but He is not. God is everywhere we have ever been and everywhere we will ever go. He is with us night and day; He knows our thoughts and our prayers. And, when we earnestly seek Him, we will find Him because He is here, waiting patiently for us to reach out to Him. May we reach out to Him today and always. And may we praise Him for the glorious gifts that have transformed us today and forever.

⌁ *Life in God is a great big hug that lasts forever!*

Barbara Johnson

⌁ *God does not love us because we are valuable. We are valuable because God loves us.*

Fulton J. Sheen

In His Hands

*Do not boast about tomorrow, for you do not know
what a day may bring forth.*

Proverbs 27:1 NKJV

The old saying is both familiar and true: "Man proposes and God disposes." Our world unfolds according to God's plans, not our wishes. Thus, boasting about future events is to be avoided by those who acknowledge God's sovereignty over all things.

Are you planning for a better tomorrow for yourself and your family? If so, you are to be congratulated: God rewards forethought in the same way that He often punishes impulsiveness. But as you make your plans, do so with humility, with gratitude, and with trust in your heavenly Father. His hand directs the future; to think otherwise is both arrogant and naïve.

That we may not complain of what is, let us see God's hand in all events; and, that we may not be afraid of what shall be, let us see all events in God's hand.

Matthew Henry

Do not limit the limitless God! With Him, face the future unafraid because you are never alone.

Mrs. Charles E. Cowman

GOD'S ASSURANCES AND YOUR CONFIDENCE

*These things I have spoken to you, that in Me you may
have peace. In the world you will have tribulation;
but be of good cheer, I have overcome the world.*

John 16:33 NKJV

⌇ Are you a confident believer, or do you live under a
cloud of uncertainty and doubt? As a Christian, you
have many reasons to be confident. After all, God
is in His heaven; Christ has risen; and you are the
recipient of God's grace. Despite these blessings, you
may, from time to time, find yourself being tormented
by negative emotions—and you are certainly not
alone.

Even the most faithful Christians are overcome
by occasional bouts of fear and doubt. You are no
different.

But even when you feel very distant from God,
remember that God is never distant from you. When
you sincerely seek His presence, He will touch your
heart, calm your fears, and restore your confidence.

⌇ *As I have grown in faith and confidence, I have known
more and more that my worth is based on the love of
God.*

Leslie Williams

COURAGE FOR THE STORMS OF LIFE

But Jesus quickly spoke to them,
"Have courage! It is I. Do not be afraid."

Matthew 14:27 NCV

❧ Sometimes, we feel threatened by the inevitable storms of life. And when we are fearful, we can turn to Jesus for courage and for comfort.

When a storm rose quickly on the Sea of Galilee, Christ's disciples were afraid. Although they had seen Jesus perform many miracles, the disciples feared for their lives, so they turned to their Savior, and He calmed the waters and the wind.

The next time you're afraid, remember that Jesus can calm the winds and the waves of your own personal storms. That means that you, as a believer whose salvation has already been purchased on the hill at Calvary, can live courageously . . . and you should.

❧ *Down through the centuries, in times of trouble and trial, God has brought courage to the hearts of those who love Him. The Bible is filled with assurances of God's help and comfort in every kind of trouble.*

Billy Graham

❧ *What is courage? It is the ability to be strong in trust, in conviction, in obedience. To be courageous is to step out in faith—to trust and obey, no matter what.*

Kay Arthur

ABOVE AND BEYOND OUR CIRCUMSTANCES

Should we take only good things from
God and not trouble?

Job 2:10 NCV

⊰ Even the most devout Christians can become discouraged, and you are no exception. After all, you live in a world where expectations can be high and demands can be even higher.

If you find yourself enduring difficult circumstances, don't lose hope. If you face uncertainties about the future, don't become anxious. And if you become discouraged with the direction of your day or your life, don't despair. Instead, lift your thoughts and prayers to your Heavenly Father. He is a God of possibility, not negativity. You can be sure that He will guide you through your difficulties and beyond them . . . far beyond.

⊰ *When you realize that your circumstances, no matter how overwhelming or pressing, are ruled by a King who seeks your highest good, you can truly "consider it all joy…when you encounter various trials, knowing that the testing of your faith produces endurance…that you may be perfect and complete, lacking in nothing" (James 1:2-4).*

Charles Swindoll

THE WISDOM TO BE HUMBLE

*When you do things, do not let selfishness or
pride be your guide. Instead, be humble and give more
honor to others than to yourselves.*

Philippians 2:3 NCV

God's Word clearly instructs us to be humble. And that's good because, as fallible human beings, we have so very much to be humble about! Yet some of us continue to puff ourselves up, seeming to say, "Look at me!" To do so is wrong.

As Christians, we have been refashioned and saved by Jesus Christ, and that salvation came not because of our own good works but because of God's grace. How, then, can we be prideful? The answer, of course, is that, if we are honest with ourselves and with our God, we simply can't be boastful...we must, instead, be eternally grateful and exceedingly humble. The good things in our lives, including our loved ones, come from God. He deserves the credit—and we deserve the glorious experience of giving it to Him.

I have learned that the more we understand how very much God loves us, and the more we comprehend the grace He has demonstrated toward us, the more humble we become.

Serita Ann Jakes

ENTHUSIASTIC SERVICE

Do your work with enthusiasm.
Work as if you were serving the Lord, not as if you were
serving only men and women.

Ephesians 6:7 NCV

❧ You are the recipient of Christ's sacrificial love. Accept it enthusiastically and share it fervently.

Do you see each day as a glorious opportunity to serve God and to do His will? Are you enthused about life, or do you struggle through each day giving scarcely a thought to God's blessings? Are you constantly praising God for His gifts, and are you sharing His Good News with the world? And are you excited about the possibilities for service that God has placed before you, whether at home, at work, at church, or at school? You should be.

Jesus deserves your enthusiasm; the world deserves it; and you deserve the experience of sharing it.

❧ *The proper perspective creates within us a spirit of reaching outside of ourselves with joy and enthusiasm.*

Luci Swindoll

❧ *One of the great needs in the church today is for every Christian to become enthusiastic about his faith in Jesus Christ.*

Billy Graham

GOD'S PLAN FOR YOUR FAMILY

If the Lord doesn't build the house, the builders are
working for nothing. If the Lord doesn't guard the city,
the guards are watching for nothing.

Psalm 127:1 NCV

A loving family is a treasure from God. If you happen to be a member of a close knit, supportive clan, offer a word of thanks to your Creator. He has blessed you with one of His most precious earthy possessions. Your obligation, in response to God's gift, is to treat your family in ways that are consistent with His commandments.

As you consider God's purpose for your own life, you must also consider how your plans will effect the most important people that God has entrusted to your care: your loved ones.

So, as you prayerfully seek God's direction, remember that He has important plans for your home life as well as your professional life. It's up to you to act—and to plan—accordingly.

It is easy to love the people far way. It is not always easy to love those close to us. It is easier to give a cup of rice to relieve hunger than to relieve the loneliness and pain of someone unloved in our own home. Bring love into your home, for this is where our love for each other must start.

Mother Teresa

An Awesome God

The fear of the Lord is a fountain of life.

Proverbs 14:27 NKJV

God's hand shapes the universe, and it shapes our lives. God maintains absolute sovereignty over His creation, and His power is beyond comprehension. As believers, we must cultivate a sincere respect for God's awesome power. God has dominion over all things, and until we acknowledge His sovereignty, we lack the humility we need to live righteously, and we lack the humility we need to become wise.

The fear of the Lord is, indeed, the beginning of knowledge. So today, as you face the realities of everyday life, remember this: until you acquire a healthy, respectful fear of God's power, your education is incomplete, and so is your faith.

When true believers are awed by the greatness of God and by the privilege of becoming His children, then they become sincerely motivated, effective evangelists.

Bill Hybels

Spiritual worship comes from our very core and is fueled by an awesome reverence and desire for God.

Beth Moore

Forgiving and Forgetting

But the wisdom that is from above is first pure,
then peaceable, gentle, willing to yield, full of mercy and
good fruits, without partiality and without hypocrisy.

James 3:17 NKJV

Do you have a tough time forgiving and forgetting? If so, welcome to the club. Most of us find it difficult to forgive the people who have hurt us. And that's too bad because life would be much simpler if we could forgive people "once and for all" and be done with it. Yet forgiveness is seldom that easy. Usually, the decision to forgive is straightforward, but the process of forgiving is more difficult. Forgiveness is a journey that requires time, perseverance, and prayer.

If you sincerely wish to forgive someone, pray for that person. And then pray for yourself by asking God to heal your heart. Don't expect forgiveness to be easy or quick, but rest assured: with God as your partner, you can forgive . . . and you will.

Forgiveness does not mean the perpetrator goes free; it means that the forgiver is free and that God will justly deal with those who have caused pain.

Cynthia Heald

There is no use in talking as if forgiveness were easy. For we find that the work of forgiveness has to be done over and over again.

C. S. Lewis

OFFERING THANKS

In everything give thanks; for this is the will of
God in Christ Jesus for you.

1 Thessalonians 5:18 NKJV

❧ Life has a way of constantly coming at us. Days, hours, and moments are filled with urgent demands requiring our immediate attention.

When the demands of life leave us rushing from place to place with scarcely a moment to spare, we may fail to pause and thank our Creator for His gifts. But, whenever we neglect to give proper thanks to the Father, we suffer because of our misplaced priorities.

Today, make a special effort to give thanks to the Creator for His blessings. His love for you is eternal, as are His gifts. And it's never too soon—or too late—to offer Him thanks.

❧ *The joy of God is experienced as I love, trust, and obey God—no matter the circumstances—and as I allow Him to do in and through me whatever He wishes, thanking Him that in every pain there is pleasure, in every suffering there is satisfaction, in every aching there is comfort, in every sense of loss there is the surety of the Savior's presence, and in every tear there is the glistening eye of God.*

Bill Bright

YOUR TALENTS, HIS CALLING

But as God has distributed to each one,
as the Lord has called each one, so let him walk.

1 Corinthians 7:17 NKJV

❧ Every believer has an assortment of gifts and talents.
In John 15:16, Jesus ssaid, "You did not choose Me,
but I chose you and appointed you that you should go
and bear fruit, and that your fruit should remain, that
whatever you ask the Father in My name He may give
you" (NKJV).

It is terribly important that you heed God's calling
by discovering and developing your talents and your
spiritual gifts. If you seek to make a difference—and if
you seek to bear eternal fruit—you must discover your
gifts and begin using them for the glory of God.

Have you found your special calling? If not, keep
searching and keep praying until you find it. God has
important work for you to do, and the time to begin
that work is now.

❧ *We can all humbly say in the sincerity of faith, "I am*
loved; I am called; I am secure."

Franklin Graham

❧ *God has given you special talents—now it's your turn to*
give them back to God.

Marie T. Freeman

A LIGHT TO THE PATH

Your word is a lamp to my feet and a light to my path.

Psalm 119:105 NKJV

⊰ The Psalmist describes God's word as, "a light to my path." Is the Bible your lamp? If not, you are depriving yourself of a priceless gift from the Creator.

Are you a person who trusts God's Word without reservation? Hopefully so, because the Bible is unlike any other book—it is a guidebook for life here on earth and for life eternal.

Vance Havner observed, "It takes calm, thoughtful, prayerful meditation on the Word to extract its deepest nourishment." How true. God's Word can be a roadmap to a place of righteous and abundance. Make it your roadmap. God's wisdom can be a light to guide your steps. Claim it as your light today, tomorrow, and every day of your life—and then walk confidently in the footsteps of God's only begotten Son.

⊰ *Our nighttime passage through the dark and dangerous journey of this life is illuminated by God's Word, the Bible: "Your word is a lamp to my feet and light for my path." It is a light for our darkness and for our brighter times as well.*

James Montgomery Boice

WAITING FOR GOD

The Lord is good to those who wait for Him,
To the soul who seeks Him. It is good that one should
hope and wait quietly For the salvation of the Lord.

Lamentations 3:25–26 NKJV

❧ We human beings are so impatient. We know what we want, and we know exactly when we want it: RIGHT NOW! But, God knows better. He has created a world that unfolds according to His own timetable, not ours.

As Christians, we must be patient as we wait for God to show us the wonderful plans that He has in store for us. And while we're waiting for God to make His plans clear, let's keep praying and keep giving thanks to the One who has given us more blessings than we can count.

❧ *Grass that is here today and gone tomorrow does not require much time to mature. A big oak tree that lasts for generations requires much more time to grow and mature. God is concerned about your life through eternity. Allow Him to take all the time He needs to shape you for His purposes. Larger assignments will require longer periods of preparation.*

Henry Blackaby

BEYOND GUILT

There is therefore now no condemnation to those who are in Christ Jesus, who do not walk according to the flesh, but according to the Spirit.

Romans 8:1 NKJV

᠔ All of us have sinned. Sometimes our sins result from our own stubborn rebellion against God's commandments. And sometimes, we are swept up in events that are beyond our abilities to control. Under either set of circumstances, we may experience intense feelings of guilt. But God has an answer for the guilt that we feel. That answer, of course, is His forgiveness. When we confess our wrongdoings and repent from them, we are forgiven by the One who created us.

Are you troubled by feelings of guilt or regret? If so, you must repent from your misdeeds, and you must ask your Heavenly Father for His forgiveness. When you do so, He will forgive you completely and without reservation. Then, you must forgive yourself just as God has forgiven you: thoroughly and unconditionally.

᠔ *You never lose the love of God. Guilt is the warning that temporarily you are out of touch.*

Jack Dominian

DREAM BIG

With God's power working in us, God can do much, much more than anything we can ask or imagine.

Ephesians 3:20 NCV

Your heavenly Father created you with unique gifts and untapped talents; your job is to tap them. When you do, you'll begin to feel an increasing sense of confidence in yourself and in your future.

Are you willing to entertain the possibility that God has big plans in store for you? Hopefully so. Yet sometimes, especially if you've recently experienced a life-altering disappointment, you may find it difficult to envision a brighter future for yourself and your family. If so, it's time to reconsider your own capabilities . . . and God's.

So even if you're experiencing difficult days, don't abandon your dreams. Instead, trust that God is preparing you for greater things.

When you affirm big, believe big, and pray big, big things happen.

Norman Vincent Peale

You pay God a compliment by asking great things of Him.

St. Teresa of Avila

THE WORLD'S BEST FRIEND

Greater love has no one than this,
than to lay down one's life for his friends.

John 15:13 NKJV

❧ Who's the best friend this world has ever had? Jesus, of course. And when you form a life-changing relationship with Him, He'll will be your best friend, too . . . your friend forever.

Jesus has offered to share the gifts of everlasting life and everlasting love with the world and with you. If you make mistakes, He'll stand by you. If you fall short of His commandments, He'll still love you. If you feel lonely or worried, He can touch your heart and lift your spirits.

Jesus wants you to enjoy a happy, healthy, abundant life. He wants you to walk with Him and to share His Good News. You can do it. And with a friend like Jesus, you will.

❧ *The dearest friend on earth is but a mere shadow compared with Jesus Christ.*

Oswald Chambers

❧ *When we are in a situation where Jesus is all we have, we soon discover he is all we really need.*

Gigi Graham Tchividjian

TOO MANY POSSESSIONS

Do not love the world or the things in the world.
If you love the world, the love of the Father is not in you.

1 John 2:15 NCV

On the grand stage of a well-lived life, material possessions should play a rather small role. Of course, we all need the basic necessities of life, but once we meet those needs for ourselves and for our families, the piling up of possessions creates more problems than it solves. Our real riches, of course, are not of this world. We are never really rich until we are rich in spirit.

How much stuff is too much stuff? Well, if your desire for stuff is getting in the way of your desire to know God, then you've got too much stuff—it's as simple as that. So, if you find yourself wrapped up in the concerns of the material world, it's time to reorder your priorities. And, it's time to begin storing up riches that will endure throughout eternity—the spiritual kind.

We are made spiritually lethargic by a steady diet of materialism.

Mary Morrison Suggs

Greed is evil because it substitutes material things for the place of honor that the Creator ought to have in an individual's life.

Charles Stanley

NEW BEGINNINGS

I will give you a new heart and put a new spirit within you.

Ezekiel 36:26 NKJV

❧ If we sincerely want to change ourselves for the better, we must start on the inside and work our way out from there. Lasting change doesn't occur "out there"; it occurs "in here." It occurs, not in the shifting sands of our own particular circumstances, but in quiet depths of our own hearts.

Are you in search of a new beginning or, for that matter, a new you? If so, don't expect changing circumstances to miraculously transform you into the person you want to become. Transformation starts with God, and it starts in the silent center of a humble human heart—like yours.

❧ *In those desperate times when we feel like we don't have an ounce of strength, He will gently pick up our heads so that our eyes can behold something—something that will keep His hope alive in us.*

Kathy Troccoli

❧ *No matter how badly we have failed, we can always get up and begin again. Our God is the God of new beginnings.*

Warren Wiersbe

GOOD PRESSURES, BAD PRESSURES

Do you think I am trying to make people accept me?
No, God is the One I am trying to please.
Am I trying to please people? If I still wanted to please
people, I would not be a servant of Christ.

Galatians 1:10 NCV

❧ Our world is filled with pressures: some good, some bad. The pressures that we feel to follow God's will and obey His commandments are positive pressures. God places them on our hearts, and He intends that we act in accordance with His leadings. But we also face different pressures, ones that are definitely not from God. When we feel pressured to do things—or even to think thoughts—that lead us away from God, we must beware.

Society seeks to mold us into more worldly beings; God seeks to mold us into new beings that are most certainly not conformed to this world. If we are to please God, we must resist the pressures that society seeks to impose upon us, and we must conform ourselves, instead, to God's will, to His path, and to His Son.

❧ *I have found that the closer I am to the godly people around me, the easier it is for me to live a righteous life because they hold me accountable.*

John MacArthur

THE IMPORTANCE OF PRAYER

*Be anxious for nothing, but in everything by prayer
and supplication, with thanksgiving,
let your requests be made known to God.*

Philippians 4:6 NKJV

⊰ Prayer is powerful tool for communicating with our Creator; it is an opportunity to commune with the Giver of all things good. Prayer is not a thing to be taken lightly or to be used infrequently. Prayer should never be reserved for mealtimes or for bedtimes; it should be an ever-present focus in our daily lives.

In his first letter to the Thessalonians, Paul wrote, "Rejoice evermore. Pray without ceasing. In every thing give thanks: for this is the will of God in Christ Jesus concerning you" (v. 5:17-18 KJV). Paul's words apply to every Christian of every generation. So, let us pray constantly about things great and small. God is listening, and He wants to hear from us. Now.

⊰ We must pray literally without ceasing, in every occurrence and employment of our lives. You know I mean that prayer of the heart which is independent of place or situation, or which is, rather, a habit of lifting up the heart to God, as in a constant communication with Him.

Elizabeth Ann Seton

THE IMPORTANCE OF SELF-CONTROL

But I discipline my body and bring it into subjection,
lest, when I have preached to others,
I myself should become disqualified.

1 Corinthians 9:27 NKJV

❧ Self-control is a virtue extolled throughout the Bible. God's Word reminds us again and again that self-discipline and patience are the hallmarks of discernment and success. But for most of us, self-control and patience can also be difficult habits to acquire.

Are you having trouble being patient? And are you having trouble slowing down long enough to think carefully before you act, not after? If so, remember that self-control takes practice, and lots of it, so don't lose hope. And if you happen to make a mistake, don't be too upset. After all, if you're going to be a really patient person, you shouldn't just be patient with others; you should also be patient with yourself.

❧ *No steam or river ever drives anything until it is confined. No Niagara is ever turned into light and power until it is harnessed. No life ever grows until it is focused, dedicated, disciplined.*

Harry Emerson Fosdick

Too Wise to be Jealous

*Where jealousy and selfishness are,
there will be confusion and every kind of evil.*

James 3:14 NCV

⍾ Are you too wise to be consumed with feelings of jealousy? Hopefully so. After all, Jesus clearly taught us to love our neighbors, not to envy them. But sometimes, despite our best intentions, we fall prey to feelings of resentfulness, jealousy, bitterness, and envy. Why? Because we are human, and because we live in a world that places great importance on material possessions (possessions which, by the way, are totally unimportant to God).

The next time you feel pangs of envy invading your thoughts, remind yourself of two things: 1. Envy is a sin, and 2. God has already showered you with so many blessings that if you're a thoughtful, thankful believer, you have no right to ever be envious of any other person on earth.

⍾ *The jealous are troublesome to others, but a torment to themselves.*

William Penn

⍾ *On the highway of life, envy is an emotional dead end.*

Anonymous

WHEN HIS RULE BECOMES YOUR RULE

And let us not grow weary while doing good,
for in due season we shall reap if we do not lose heart.

Galatians 6:9 NKJV

❧ Would you like to make the world a better place and feel better about yourself at the same time? If so, you can start by practicing the Golden Rule.

The Bible teaches us to treat other people with respect, kindness, courtesy, and love. When we do, we make other people happy, we make God happy, and we naturally feel better about ourselves.

So if you're wondering how to make the world— and your world—a better place, here's a great place to start: let the Golden Rule be your rule. And if you want to know how to treat other people, ask the person you see every time you glance in the mirror. The answer you receive will tell you precisely what to do.

❧ *Sometimes one little spark of kindness is all it takes to reignite the light of hope in a heart that's blinded by pain.*

Barbara Johnson

❧ *When you launch an act of kindness out into the crosswinds of life, it will blow kindness back to you.*

Dennis Swanberg

WALK IN TRUTH

But when the Spirit of truth comes,
he will lead you into all truth.

John 16:13 NCV

❧ The familiar words of John 8:32 remind us that "you shall know the truth, and the truth shall make you free" (NKJV). And St. Augustine had this advice: "Let everything perish! Dismiss these empty vanities! And let us take up the search for the truth."

God is vitally concerned with truth. His Word teaches the truth; His Spirit reveals the truth; His Son leads us to the truth. When we open our hearts to God, and when we allow His Son to rule over our thoughts and our lives, God reveals Himself, and we come to understand the truth about ourselves and the Truth about God's gift of grace.

Are you seeking the truth and living by it? Hopefully so. When you do, you'll discover that the truth will indeed set you free, now and forever.

❧ *Truth will triumph. The Father of truth will win, and the followers of truth will be saved.*

Max Lucado

❧ *Those who walk in truth walk in liberty.*

Beth Moore

THY WILL BE DONE

Shouldn't I drink the cup the Father gave me?

John 18:11 NCV

❧ All of us must, from time to time, endure days filled with suffering and pain. And as human beings with limited understanding, we can never fully understand the plans of our Father in Heaven. But as believers in a benevolent God, we must always trust Him.

When Jesus went to the Mount of Olives, He poured out His heart to God (Luke 22). Jesus knew of the agony that He was destined to endure, but He also knew that God's will must be done.

When we face circumstances that shake us to the depths of our souls, we, like Christ, must seek God's will, not our own. When we learn to accept God's will without reservation, we will, in time, come to experience the peace that the Father offers to wise believers (like you) who trust Him completely.

❧ *The will of God for your life is simply that you submit yourself to Him each day and say, "Father, Your will for today is mine. Your pleasure for today is mine. Your work for today is mine. I trust You to be God. You lead me today and I will follow."*

Kay Arthur

HE HEALS

I have heard your prayer, I have seen your tears;
surely I will heal you.

2 Kings 20:5 NKJV

❧ Jesus overcame the world, and He promised that we can overcome it, too. But sometimes, we really don't feel strong enough to overcome anything. Sometimes we experience life-changing personal losses that leave us felling downhearted, discouraged or worse. When we do, we should remember Christ's assurances, and we should remember that God stands ready to protect us. When we are deeply troubled, we must call upon God, and then, in His own time and according to His own plan, He will heal us.

Are you anxious? Take those anxieties to God. Are you troubled? Take your troubles to Him. Does your world seem to be trembling beneath your feet? Seek protection from the One who cannot be moved. The same God who created the universe will protect you if you ask Him...so ask Him.

❧ *Looking back, my wife Jan and I have learned that the wilderness is part of the landscape of faith, and every bit as essential as the mountaintop. On the mountaintop, we are overwhelmed by God's presence. In the wilderness, we are overwhelmed by his absence. Both places should bring us to our knees; the one in utter awe; the other in utter dependence.*

Dave Dravecky

WHEN PEOPLE BEHAVE BADLY

Don't make friends with quick-tempered people or
spend time with those who have bad tempers. If you do,
you will be like them. Then you will be in real danger.

Proverbs 22:24-25 NCV

❦ Face it: sometimes people can be difficult to deal with . . . very, very difficult. When other people are unkind to you, you may be tempted to strike back, either verbally or in some other way. Resist that temptation. Instead, remember that God corrects other people's behaviors in His own way, and He doesn't need your help (even if you're totally convinced that He does).

So when other people behave cruelly, foolishly, or impulsively—as they will from time to time—don't respond in kind. Instead, speak up for yourself as politely as you can, and walk away. Then, forgive everybody as quickly as you can and leave the rest up to God.

❦ *You can be sure you are abiding in Christ if you are able to have a Christlike love toward the people that irritate you the most.*

Vonette Bright

❦ *We are all fallen creatures and all very hard to live with.*

C. S. Lewis

MAKING PEACE WITH YOUR PAST

Forget what happened before, and do not think about
the past. Look at the new thing I am going to do.
It is already happening. Don't you see it? I will make
a road in the desert and rivers in the dry land.

Isaiah 43:18-19 NCV

❧ Dennis Swanberg had this advice: "Don't be intimidated by your past, good or bad. Face it, deal with it and then get over it and let it go. Begin a new day and new tradition for those who follow after you."

Have you made peace with your past? If so, congratulations. But, if you are mired in the quicksand of regret, it's time to plan your escape. How can you do so? By accepting what has been and by trusting God for what will be.

Because you are human, you may be slow to forget yesterday's disappointments. But, if you sincerely seek to focus your hopes and energies on the future, then you must find ways to accept the past, no matter how difficult it may be to do so. So, if you have not yet made peace with the past, today is the day to declare an end to all hostilities. When you do, you can then turn your thoughts to wondrous promises of God and to the glorious future that He has in store for you.

❧ *We can't just put our pasts behind us. We've got to put our pasts in front of God.*

Beth Moore

REJOICE!

Rejoice in the Lord always. Again I will say, rejoice!
Philippians 4:4 NKJV

❧ Today, let us celebrate life as God intended. Today, let us share the Good News of Jesus Christ. Today, let us put smiles on our faces, kind words on our lips, and songs in our hearts. Let us be generous with our praise and free with our encouragement.

Oswald Chambers correctly observed, "Joy is the great note all throughout the Bible." C. S. Lewis echoed that thought when he wrote, "Joy is the serious business of heaven." But, even the most dedicated Christians can, on occasion, forget to celebrate each day for what it is: a priceless gift from God.

So let us celebrate life to the fullest, and let us invite others to do likewise. After all, this is God's day, and He has given us clear instructions for its use. We are commanded to rejoice and be glad. So, with no further ado, let the celebration begin...

❧ *If you can forgive the person you were, accept the person you are, and believe in the person you will become, you are headed for joy. So celebrate your life.*
Barbara Johnson

❧ *I know nothing, except what everyone knows—if there where God dances, I should dance.*
W. H. Auden

THE GIFT OF CHEERFULNESS

Worry is a heavy load, but a kind word cheers you up.

Proverbs 12:25 NCV

❧ Cheerfulness is a gift that we give to others and to ourselves. As believers who have been saved by a risen Christ, why shouldn't we be cheerful? The answer, of course, is that we have every reason to honor our Savior with joy in our hearts, smiles on our faces, and words of celebration on our lips.

Christ promises us lives of abundance and joy if we accept His love and His grace. Yet sometimes, even the most righteous among us are beset by fits of ill temper and frustration. During these moments, we may not feel like turning our thoughts and prayers to Christ, but that's precisely what we should do. When we do so, we simply can't stay grumpy for long.

❧ *Cheerfulness prepares a glorious mind for all the noblest acts of religion—love, adoration, praise, and every union with our God.*

St. Elizabeth Ann Seton

❧ *Make each day useful and cheerful and prove that you know the worth of time by employing it well. Then youth will be happy, old age without regret, and life a beautiful success.*

Louisa May Alcott

CONTENTMENT THAT LASTS

*Serving God does make us very rich, if we are satisfied
with what we have. We brought nothing into the world,
so we can take nothing out. But, if we have food
and clothes, we will be satisfied with that.*

1 Timothy 6:6–8 NCV

❧ The preoccupation with happiness and contentment is an ever-present theme in our modern world. We are bombarded with messages that tell us where to find peace and pleasure in a world that worships materialism and wealth.

The world promises to give us contentment through worldly means: wealth, fame, power, and status. But the world is wrong—material possessions and social standing have precious little to do with lasting happiness.

Genuine contentment is a spiritual gift from God to those who trust in Him and follow His commandments. When God dwells at the center of our lives, peace and contentment will belong to us just as surely as we belong to God.

❧ *If I could just hang in there, being faithful to my own tasks, God would make me joyful and content. The responsibility is mine, but the power is His.*

Peg Rankin

LISTENING TO THE VOICE

People's thoughts can be like a deep well, but someone with understanding can find the wisdom there.

Proverbs 20:5 NCV

❧ God gave you a conscience for a very good reason: to make your path conform to His will. Billy Graham correctly observed, "Most of us follow our conscience as we follow a wheelbarrow. We push it in front of us in the direction we want to go." To do so, of course, is a profound mistake. Yet all of us, on occasion, have failed to listen to the voice that God planted in our hearts, and all of us have suffered the consequences.

Wise believers make it a practice to listen carefully to that quiet internal voice. Count yourself among that number. When your conscience speaks, listen and learn. In all likelihood, God is trying to get His message through. And in all likelihood, it is a message that you desperately need to hear.

❧ *Whatever weakens your reason, impairs the tenderness of your conscience, obscures your sense of God, or removes your relish for spiritual things—that is sin to you.*

Susanna Wesley

❧ *Many words do not satisfy the soul; but a good life eases the mind and a clean conscience inspires great trust in God.*

Thomas à Kempis

THE NEED FOR SELF-DISCIPLINE

*Do you not know that those who run in a race all run,
but one receives the prize? Run in such a way that you
may obtain it. And everyone who competes for the prize
is temperate in all things. Now they do it to obtain
a perishable crown, but we for an imperishable crown.*

1 Corinthians 9:24–25 NKJV

❦ The words disciple and discipline are both derived
from Latin, so it's not surprising that when you become
a disciple of Christ you should expect to exercise self-
discipline in all matters. Self-discipline is not simply
a proven way to get ahead, it's also an integral part of
God's plan for your life. So if you genuinely seek to be
a faithful steward of your time, your talents, and your
resources, you must adopt a disciplined approach to
life. Otherwise, your talents are likely to go unused,
and your resources are likely to be squandered.

Most of life's greatest rewards come as the result of
hard work and perseverance. May you, as a disciplined
disciple, be willing to do the work—and keep doing
it—until you've earned the rewards that God has in
store for you.

❦ *The alternative to discipline is disaster.*

Vance Havner

❦ *There is no influence so powerful as that of a mother.*

Sarah J. Hale

STANDING UP FOR YOUR FAITH

Watch, stand fast in the faith, be brave, be strong.

1 Corinthians 16:13 NKJV

❧ Genuine faith is never meant to be locked up in the heart of a believer; to the contrary, it is meant to be shared with the world. But, if you sincerely seek to share your faith, you must first find it.

Every life—including yours—is a series of successes and failures, celebrations and disappointments, joys and sorrows. Every step of the way, through every triumph and tragedy, God will stand by your side and strengthen you . . . if you have faith in Him.

As your faith becomes stronger, you will find ways to share it with your friends, your family, and with the world. When you place your faith, your trust, indeed your life in the hands of Christ Jesus, you'll be amazed at the marvelous things He can do with you and through you; so trust God's plans. With Him, all things are possible, and He stands ready to open a world of possibilities to you . . . if you have faith.

❧ *Talk faith. The world is better off without your uttered ignorance and morbid doubt. If you have faith in God, or man, or self, say so. If not, push back upon the shelf of silence all your thoughts, till faith shall come; no one will grieve because your lips are dumb.*

Ella Wheeler Wilcox

TODAY'S OPPORTUNITIES TO ENCOURAGE

But encourage each other every day while it is "today."
Help each other so none of you will become hardened
because sin has tricked you.

Hebrews 3:13 NCV

❦ Each day provides countless opportunities to encourage others and to praise their good works. When we do, we not only spread seeds of joy and happiness, we also follow the commandments of God's Holy Word.

How can we build others up? By celebrating their victories and their accomplishments. So look for the good in others and celebrate the good that you find. When you do, you'll be a powerful force of encouragement in the world...and a worthy servant to your God.

❦ *If someone listens or stretches out a hand or whispers a word of encouragement or attempts to understand a lonely person, extraordinary things begin to happen.*

Loretta Girzartis

❦ *Those who keep speaking about the sun while walking under a cloudy sky are messengers of hope, the true saints of our day.*

Henri J. Nouwen

A PASSION FOR LIFE

But those who wait on the LORD
Shall renew their strength; They shall mount up with
wings like eagles, They shall run and not be weary,
They shall walk and not faint.

Isaiah 40:31 NKJV

❧ If your enthusiasm for life has waned, it is now time to redirect your efforts and recharge your spiritual batteries. And that means refocusing your priorities (by putting God first) and counting your blessings (instead of your troubles).

Nothing is more important than your wholehearted commitment to your Creator and to His only begotten Son. Your faith must never be an afterthought; it must be your ultimate priority, your ultimate possession, and your ultimate passion. When you become passionate about your faith, you'll become passionate about your life, too. And God will smile.

❧ *Don't take hold of a thing unless you want that thing to take hold of you.*

E. Stanley Jones

❧ *If your heart has grown cold, it is because you have moved away from the fire of His presence.*

Beth Moore

ASK AND RECEIVE

Ask, and it will be given to you; seek, and you will find;
knock, and it will be opened to you. For everyone
who asks receives, and he who seeks finds,
and to him who knocks it will be opened.

Matthew 7:7-8 NKJV

❧ Jesus made it clear to His disciples: they should petition God to meet their needs. So should we. Genuine, heartfelt prayer produces powerful changes in us and in our world. When we lift our hearts to God, we open ourselves to a never-ending source of divine wisdom and infinite love.

Do you have questions about your future that you simply can't answer? Do you have needs that you simply can't meet by yourself? Do you sincerely seek to know God's purpose for your life? If so, ask Him for direction, for protection, and for strength—and then keep asking Him every day that you live. Whatever your need, no matter how great or small, pray about it and never lose hope. God is not just near; He is here, and He's perfectly capable of answering your prayers. Now, it's up to you to ask.

❧ *God makes prayer as easy as possible for us. He's completely approachable and available, and He'll never mock or upbraid us for bringing our needs before Him.*

Shirley Dobson

FORGIVENESS AT HOME

Let all bitterness, wrath, anger, clamor, and evil speaking
be put away from you, with all malice. And be kind to
one another, tenderhearted, forgiving one another,
just as God in Christ forgave you.

Ephesians 4:31-32 NKJV

❧ Sometimes, it's easy to become angry with the people we love most, and sometimes it's hard to forgive them. After all, we know that our family will still love us no matter how angry we become. But while it's easy to become angry at home, it's usually wrong.

The next time you're tempted to lose your temper or to remain angry at a close family member, ask God to help you find the wisdom to forgive. And while you're at it, do your best to calm down sooner rather than later because peace is always beautiful, especially when it's peace at your house.

❧ *When something robs you of your peace of mind, ask yourself if it is worth the energy you are expending on it. If not, then put it out of your mind in an act of discipline. Every time the thought of "it" returns, refuse it.*

Kay Arthur

❧ *The fire of anger, if not quenched by loving forgiveness, will spread and defile and destroy the work of God.*

Warren Wiersbe

BEYOND ANXIETY

In the multitude of my anxieties within me,
Your comforts delight my soul.

Psalm 94:19 NKJV

❧ Sometimes, trusting God is difficult, especially when we become caught up in the incessant demands of an anxious world. God calls us to live above and beyond anxiety. God calls us to live by faith, not by fear. He instructs us to trust Him completely, this day and forever.

When you feel anxious—and you will—return your thoughts to God's love. Then, take your concerns to Him in prayer, and to the best of your ability, leave them there. Whatever "it" is, God is big enough to handle it. Let Him. Now.

❧ *The moment anxious thoughts invade your mind, go to the Lord in prayer. Look first to God. Then, you will see the cause of your anxiety in a whole new light.*

Kay Arthur

❧ *Worry and anxiety are sand in the machinery of life; faith is the oil.*

E. Stanley Jones

❧ *Anxiety is the natural result when our hopes are centered on anything short of God and His will for us.*

Billy Graham

A Terrific Tomorrow

*"I say this because I know what I am planning for you,"
says the Lord. "I have good plans for you, not plans to
hurt you. I will give you hope and a good future."*

Jeremiah 29:11 NCV

❧ How bright do you believe your future to be? Well,
if you're a faithful believer, God has plans for you that
are so bright that you'd better pack several pairs of
sunglasses and a lifetime supply of sunblock!

The way that you think about your future will play
a powerful role in determining how things turn out
(it's called the "self-fulfilling prophecy", and it applies
to everybody, including you). So here's another
question: Are you expecting a terrific tomorrow, or
are you dreading a terrible one? The answer to that
question will have a powerful impact on the way
tomorrow unfolds.

Today, as you live in the present and look to the
future, remember that God has an amazing plan for
you. Act—and believe—accordingly. And one more
thing: don't forget the sunblock.

❧ *No matter how heavy the burden, daily strength is given,
so I expect we need not give ourselves any concern as to
what the outcome will be. We must simply go forward.*

Annie Armstrong

AN ATTITUDE OF GRATITUDE

*And let the peace of God rule in your hearts,
to which also you were called in one body;
and be thankful.*

Colossians 3:15 NKJV

❧ The beat goes on . . . and on . . . and on . . . . Yes,
life is both busy and complicated. We have countless
responsibilities, some of which begin before sunrise
and many of which end long after sunset. Amid the
rush and crush of the daily grind, it is easy to lose
sight of God and His blessings. But, when we forget to
slow down and say "Thank You" to our Maker, we rob
ourselves of His presence, His peace, and His joy.

Our task, as believing Christians, is to praise
God many times each day. Then, with gratitude
in our hearts, we can face our daily duties with the
perspective and power that only He can provide.

❧ *It is only with gratitude that life becomes rich.*

Dietrich Bonhoeffer

❧ *A sense of gratitude for God's presence in our lives will
help open our eyes to what he has done in the past and
what he will do in the future.*

Emilie Barnes

ADDITIONAL RESPONSIBILITIES

So he who had received five talents came and brought
five other talents, saying, "Lord, you delivered to me
five talents; look, I have gained five more talents besides
them." His lord said to him, "Well done, good and
faithful servant; you were faithful over a few things,
I will make you ruler over many things.
Enter into the joy of your lord."

Matthew 25:20-21 NKJV

❧ God has promised us this: when we do our duties in small matters, He will give us additional responsibilities. Sometimes, those responsibilities come when God changes the course of our lives so that we may better serve Him. Sometimes, our rewards come in the form of temporary setbacks that lead, in turn, to greater victories. Sometimes, God rewards us by answering "no" to our prayers so that He can say "yes" to a far grander request that we, with our limited understanding, would never have thought to ask for.

If you seek to be God's servant in great matters, be faithful, be patient, and be dutiful in smaller matters. Then step back and watch as God surprises you with the spectacular creativity of His infinite wisdom and His perfect plan.

❧ *Employ whatever God has entrusted you with, in doing good, all possible good, in every possible kind and degree.*

John Wesley

Relying Upon Him

*Be humble under God's powerful hand so he will
lift you up when the right time comes. Give all your
worries to him, because he cares about you.*

1 Peter 5:6-7 NCV

❧ Do the demands of this day threaten to overwhelm
you? If so, you must rely not only upon your own
resources but also upon the promises of your Father
in heaven. God is a never-ending source of support
and courage for those of us who call upon Him. When
we are weary, He gives us strength. When we see no
hope, God reminds us of His promises. When we
grieve, God wipes away our tears.

God will hold your hand and walk with you
every day of your life if you let Him. So even if your
circumstances are difficult, trust the Father. His love
is eternal and His goodness endures forever.

❧ *Snuggle in God's arms. When you are hurting, when
you feel lonely or left out, let Him cradle you, comfort
you, reassure you of His all-sufficient power and love.*

Kay Arthur

❧ *Whatever may be our circumstances in life, may each
one of us really believe that by way of the Throne we have
unlimited power.*

Annie Armstrong

HIS COMFORTING HAND

*Nevertheless God, who comforts the downcast,
comforted us . . . .*

2 Corinthians 7:6 NKJV

❧ Jesus has won the victory, so all Christians should live courageously, including you. If you have been touched by the transforming hand of God's Son, then you have every reason to be confident about your future here on earth and your future in heaven. But even if you are a faithful believer, you may find yourself discouraged by the inevitable disappointments and tragedies that are the price of life here on earth.

If your courage is being tested today, lean upon God's promises. Trust His Son. Remember that God is always near and that He is your protector and your deliverer. When you are worried, anxious, or afraid, call upon Him and accept the touch of His comforting hand. Remember that God rules both mountaintops and valleys—with limitless wisdom and love—now and forever.

❧ *When I am criticized, injured, or afraid, there is a Father who is ready to comfort me.*

Max Lucado

❧ *Put your hand into the hand of God. He gives the calmness and serenity of heart and soul.*

Mrs. Charles E. Cowman

The Best Policy

The goodness of the innocent makes life easier,
but the wicked will be destroyed by their wickedness.

Proverbs 11:5 NCV

❧ For Christians, the issue of honesty is not a topic for debate. Honesty is not just the best policy, it is God's policy, pure and simple.

From the time we are children, we are taught that honesty is the best policy, but sometimes, being honest is hard. So, we convince ourselves that it's alright to tell "little white lies." But there's a problem: Little white lies tend to grow up, and when they do, they cause havoc and pain in our lives.

If we are to be servants worthy of our Savior, Jesus Christ, we must avoid all lies, white or otherwise. So, if you're tempted to sow the seeds of deception (perhaps in the form of a "harmless" white lie), resist that temptation. Truth is God's way, and a lie—of whatever color—is not.

❧ *God doesn't expect you to be perfect, but he does insist on complete honesty.*

Rick Warren

❧ *Much guilt arises in the life of the believer from practicing the chameleon life of environmental adaptation.*

Beth Moore

THE BREAD OF LIFE

Then Jesus said, "I am the bread that gives life.
Whoever comes to me will never be hungry,
and whoever believes in me will never be thirsty."

John 6:35 NCV

❧ Jesus Christ, the Son of God, was born into humble circumstances. He walked this earth, not as a ruler of men, but as the Savior of mankind. He was the Son of God, but He wore a crown of thorns. He was the Savior of mankind, yet He was put to death on roughhewn cross made of wood. He offered His healing touch to an unsaved world, and yet the same hands that had healed the sick and raised the dead were pierced with nails.

His crucifixion, a torturous punishment that was intended to end His life and His reign, instead became the pivotal event in the history of all humanity.

Jesus is the bread of life. Accept His grace. Share His love. And follow in His footsteps.

❧ *Our Lord is the Bread of Life. His proportions are perfect. There never was too much or too little of anything about Him. Feed on Him for a well-balanced ration. All the vitamins and calories are there.*

Vance Havner

❧ *Jesus was the perfect reflection of God's nature in every situation He encountered during His time here on earth.*

Bill Hybels

LOVE IS A CHOICE

Beloved, if God so loved us,
we also ought to love one another.

1 John 4:11 NKJV

❧ The decision to love another person for a lifetime is much more than the simple process of "falling in" or "being swept up." Sometimes, of course, we may "fall in love," but it takes work to stay there. Sometimes, we may be "swept off our feet," but the "sweeping" is only temporary; sooner or later, if love is to endure, one must plant one's feet firmly on the ground.

Love requires "reaching out," "holding firm," and "lifting up." Love, then, becomes a decision to honor and care for the other person, come what may. Love, simply put, is a choice.

❧ *How do you spell love? When you reach the point where the happiness, security, and development of another person is as much of a driving force to you as your own happiness, security, and development, then you have a mature love. True love is spelled G-I-V-E.*

Josh McDowell

❧ *A soul cannot live without loving. It must have something to love, for it was created to love.*

Catherine of Siena

A FUTURE FILLED WITH OPPORTUNITIES

Be wise in the way you act with people who are not believers, making the most of every opportunity.

Colossians 4:5 NCV

❧ If you trust God's promises, and if you have welcomed God's Son into your heart, then you believe that your future is intensely and eternally bright—and as a consequence of your beliefs, you should be excited about the opportunities of today and thrilled by the possibilities of tomorrow. You should confidently expect God to lead you to a place of abundance, peace, and joy. And, when your days on earth are over, you should expect to receive the priceless gift of eternal life.

Today, as you prepare to meet the duties of everyday life, pause and consider God's promises. And then think for a moment about the wonderful future that awaits all believers, including you. God has promised that your future is secure. Trust that promise, and celebrate the life of abundance and eternal joy that is now yours through Christ.

❧ *Worry is the senseless process of cluttering up tomorrow's opportunities with leftover problems from today.*

Barbara Johnson

AT PEACE WITH YOUR PURPOSE

But now in Christ Jesus you who once were far off
have been brought near by the blood of Christ.
For He Himself is our peace.

Ephesians 2:13–14 NKJV

❧ Are you at peace with the direction of your life? If you're a Christian, you should be. Perhaps you seek a new direction or a sense of renewed purpose, but those feelings should never rob you of the genuine peace that can and should be yours through a personal relationship with Jesus.

Have you found the lasting peace that can be yours through Jesus, or are you still rushing after the illusion of "peace and happiness" that our world promises but cannot deliver? Today, as a gift to yourself, to your family, and to your friends, claim the inner peace that is your spiritual birthright: the peace of Jesus Christ.

❧ *That peace, which has been described and which believers enjoy, is a participation of the peace which their glorious Lord and Master himself enjoys.*

Jonathan Edwards

❧ *Let's please God by actively seeking, through prayer, "peaceful and quiet lives" for ourselves, our spouses, our children and grandchildren, our friends, and our nation.*

Shirley Dobson

THE POWER OF PRAYER

When a believing person prays, great things happen.

James 5:16 NCV

❧ Prayer is powerful tool for communicating with our Creator; it is an opportunity to commune with the Giver of all things good. Prayer helps us find strength for today and hope for the future. Prayer is not a thing to be taken lightly or to be used infrequently.

The quality of your spiritual life will be in direct proportion to the quality of your prayer life. Prayer changes things, and it changes you. Today, instead of turning things over in your mind, turn them over to God in prayer. Instead of worrying about your next decision, ask God to lead the way. Pray constantly about things great and small. God is listening, and He wants to hear from you now.

❧ *Where there is much prayer, there will be much of the Spirit; where there is much of the Spirit, there will be ever-increasing power.*

Andrew Murray

❧ *The greatest power that God has given to any individual is the power of prayer.*

Kathryn Kuhlman

MAKING TIME FOR SILENCE

Be still, and know that I am God.

Psalm 46:10 NKJV

❧ Silence may indeed be golden, but it is hard for most of us to remain silent for long. God teaches us that it takes stillness to know Him. But stillness is hard.

Do you take time each day for an extended period of silence? And during those precious moments, do you sincerely open your heart to your Creator? If so, you are wise and you are blessed.

This world can be a noisy place, a place filled to the brim with distractions, interruptions, and frustrations. And if you're not careful, the struggles and stresses of everyday living can rob you of the peace that should rightfully be yours because of your personal relationship with Christ. So take time each day to quietly commune with your Savior. When you do, those moments of silence will enable you to participate more fully in the only source of peace that endures: God's peace.

❧ *Most of man's trouble comes from his inability to be still.*

Blaise Pascal

❧ *The world is full of noise. Might we not set ourselves to learn silence, stillness, solitude?*

Elisabeth Elliot

STANDING ON THE ROCK

He heals the brokenhearted and bandages their wounds.

Psalm 147:3 NCV

❧ God loves us and protects us. In times of trouble, he is willing to comfort us; in times of sorrow, He is willing to dry our tears. So when we are troubled, we must call upon God, and—in His own time and according to His own plan—He will heal us.

Do you feel fearful, or weak, or sorrowful? Are you discouraged or bitter? Do you feel "stuck" in a place that is uncomfortable for you? If so, remember that God is as near as your next breath. So trust Him and turn to Him for solace, for security, and for salvation. And build your life on the rock that cannot be shaken . . . that rock is God.

❧ *He is within and without. His Spirit dwells within me. His armor protects me. He goes before me and is behind me.*

Mary Morrison Suggs

❧ *If the Father knows when a sparrow falls, don't you think He's aware of where you are, what your need is, and what your concern is? Rest in that.*

Jack Hayford

❧ *A mighty fortress is our God.*

Martin Luther

WORSHIP HIM

*God is spirit, and those who worship him must
worship in spirit and truth.*

John 4:24 NCV

❊ What will you choose to worship today? Will you worship your Creator or your possessions? Will you worship your Savior, Jesus Christ, or will you bow down before the false gods of pride and avarice? Will you seek the approval of your God or the approval of your neighbors?

All of mankind is engaged in the practice of worship. Some people choose to worship God and, as a result, reap the joy that He intends for His children. Others distance themselves from God by worshiping such things as earthly possessions or personal gratification…and when they do, they suffer.

Every day provides opportunities to put God where He belongs: at the center of your life. Worship Him—and only Him—today, tomorrow, and always.

❊ *Worship is a way of living, a way of seeing the world in the light of God. To worship is to rise to a higher level of existence, to see the world from the point of view of God.*

Abraham Joshua Heschel

❊ *God asks that we worship Him with our concentrated minds as well as with our wills and emotions. A divided and scattered mind is not effective.*

Catherine Marshall

A HELPING HAND

Then a Samaritan traveling down the road came to where the hurt man was. When he saw the man, he felt very sorry for him. The Samaritan went to him, poured olive oil and winen on his wounds, and bandaged them. Then he put the hurt man on his own donkey and took him to an inn where he cared for him.

Luke 10:33-34 NCV

❋ Sometimes we would like to help make the world a better place, but we're not sure how to do it. Jesus told the story of the "Good Samaritan," a man who helped a fellow traveler when no one else would. We, too, should be good Samaritans when we find people who need our help.

What can you do to make God's world a better place? You can start by making your own corner of the world a little nicer place to live (by sharing kind words and good deeds). And then, you can take your concerns to God in prayer. Whether you've offered a helping hand or a heartfelt prayer, you've done a lot.

❋ *Do all the good you can. By all the means you can. In all the ways you can. In all the places you can. At all the times you can. To all the people you can. As long as ever you can.*

John Wesley

YOUR PLANS AND GOD'S PLANS

People may make plans in their minds,
but the Lord decides what they will do.

Proverbs 16:9 NCV

❋ It's time to trust God completely. And it's time to reclaim the peace—His peace—that can and should be yours. If you're like most people, you like being in control. Period. You want things to happen according to your wishes and according to your timetable. But sometimes, God has other plans . . . and He always has the final word.

So if you've encountered unfortunate circumstances that are beyond your power to control, accept those circumstances . . . and trust God. When you do, you can be comforted in the knowledge that your Creator is both loving and wise, and that He understands His plans perfectly, even when you do not.

❋ *Faith in God will not get for you everything you want, but it will get for you what God wants you to have. The unbeliever does not need what he wants; the Christian should want only what he needs.*

Vance Havner

❋ *Loving Him means the thankful acceptance of all things that His love has appointed.*

Elisabeth Elliot

THE WISDOM TO FORGIVE

Get along with each other, and forgive each other.
If someone does wrong to you, forgive that person
because the Lord forgave you.

Colossians 3:13 NCV

❧ Whenever people hurt us—whether emotionally, physically, financially, or otherwise—it's hard to forgive. But God's Word is clear: we must forgive other people, even when we'd rather not. So, if you're angry with anybody (or if you're upset by something you yourself have done) it's now time to forgive.

God instructs you to treat other people exactly as you wish to be treated. And since you want to be forgiven for the mistakes that you make, you must be willing to extend forgiveness to other people for the mistakes that they have made.

If you can't seem to forgive someone, you should keep asking God for help you until you do. And of this you can be sure: if you keep asking for God's help, He will give it.

❧ *Have you thought that your willingness to forgive is really your affirmation of the power of God to do you good?*

Paula Rinehart

❧ *Having forgiven, I am liberated.*

Father Lawrence Jenco

DIRECTING YOUR THOUGHTS

My cup runs over. Surely goodness and mercy shall follow me all the days of my life; and I will dwell in the house of the Lord Forever.

Psalm 23:5-6 NKJV

❧ The quality of your attitude will help determine the quality of your life, so you must guard your thoughts accordingly. Here's how God wants you to direct those thoughts: "Finally, brethren, whatever things are true, whatever things are noble, whatever things are just, whatever things are pure, whatever things are lovely, whatever things are of good report, if there is any virtue and if there is anything praiseworthy— meditate on these things." (Philippians 4:8 NKJV)

If you make up your mind to approach life with a healthy mixture of realism and optimism, you'll be rewarded. But, if you allow yourself to fall into the unfortunate habit of negative thinking, you will doom yourself to unhappiness, or mediocrity, or worse. So, the next time you find yourself dwelling upon the negative aspects of your life, refocus your attention on things positive. And remember: You'll never whine your way to the top . . . so don't waste your time trying.

❧ *Developing a positive attitude means working continually to find what is uplifting and encouraging.*

Barbara Johnson

BREAD IS NEVER ENOUGH

Man shall not live by bread alone, but by every word
that proceeds from the mouth of God.

Matthew 4:4 NKJV

❧ The Bible is a priceless gift, a tool for Christians to use as they share the Good News of their Savior, Christ Jesus. Too many Christians, however, keep their Bibles tightly closed collecting dust.

Jonathan Edwards advised, "Be assiduous in reading the Holy Scriptures. This is the fountain whence all knowledge in divinity must be derived. Therefore let not this treasure lie by you neglected." And he was right.

God's Holy Word is, indeed, a priceless, one-of-a-kind treasure. Treat it with respect, read it every day . . . because neither man nor woman should live by bread alone.

❧ *Decisions which are made in the light of God's Word are stable and show wisdom.*

Vonette Bright

❧ *The Bible is the treasure map that leads us to God's highest treasure: eternal life.*

Max Lucado

A GROWING RELATIONSHIP WITH GOD

But grow in the grace and knowledge of our Lord and Savior Jesus Christ. To Him be the glory both now and forever.

2 Peter 3:18 NKJV

※ Are you continuing to grow in your love and knowledge of the Lord, or are you "satisfied" with the current state of your spiritual health? Your relationship with God is ongoing; it unfolds day by day, and it offers countless opportunities to grow closer to Him . . . or not.

As each new day unfolds, you are confronted with a wide range of decisions: how you will behave, where you will direct your thoughts, with whom you will associate, and what you will choose to worship. These choices, along with many others like them, are yours and yours alone. How you choose determines how your relationship with God will unfold.

Hopefully, you're determined make yourself a growing Christian. Your Savior deserves no less, and neither, by the way, do you.

※ *When it comes to walking with God, there is no such thing as instant maturity. God doesn't mass produce His saints. He hand tools each one, and it always takes longer than we expected.*

Charles Swindoll

How Cheerful?

Be of good comfort, be of one mind, live in peace;
and the God of love and peace will be with you.

2 Corinthians 13:11 NKJV

❋ Are you a really cheerful Christian? You should be! John Wesley correctly observed, "Sour godliness is the devil's religion." These words remind us that pessimism and doubt are some of the most important tools that Satan uses to achieve his objectives. Our challenge, of course, is to ensure that Satan cannot use these tools on us.

Mrs. Charles E. Cowman, the author of the classic devotional text, *Streams in the Desert*, wrote, "Two wings are necessary to lift our souls toward God: prayer and praise. Prayer asks. Praise accepts the answer." That's why we should find the time to lift our concerns to God in prayer, and to praise Him for all that He has done. And what is the best way to attain the joy that is rightfully yours? By giving Christ what is rightfully His: your heart, your soul, and your life.

❋ *God is good, and heaven is forever. And if those two facts don't cheer you up, nothing will.*

Marie T. Freeman

❋ *Be merry, really merry. The life of a true Christian should be a perpetual jubilee, a prelude to the festivals of eternity.*

Theophare Venard

GIVING YOUR WORRIES TO GOD

*Be humble under God's powerful hand so he will lift
you up when the right time comes. Give all your worries
to him, because he cares about you.*

1 Peter 5:6-7 NCV

❋ Perhaps you are uncertain about your future—or
perhaps you are simply a "worrier" by nature. If so, it's
time to focus less on your troubles and more on God's
promises. And that's as it should be because God is
trustworthy…and you are protected.

If you are a person with lots of obligations and
plenty of responsibilities, it is simply a fact of life:
You worry. From time to time, you worry about
health, about finances, about safety, about family,
and about countless other concerns, some great and
some small.

Where is the best place to take your worries? Take
them to God. Take your troubles to Him; take your
fears to Him; take your doubts to Him; take your
weaknesses to Him; take your sorrows to Him . . . and
leave them all there. Seek protection from the One
who offers you eternal salvation; build your spiritual
house upon the Rock that cannot be moved.

❋ *Don't take tomorrow to bed with you.*

Norman Vincent Peale

A CLEAR CONSCIENCE

If then you were raised with Christ, seek those things which are above, where Christ is, sitting at the right hand of God. Set your mind on things above, not on things on the earth.

Colossians 3:1-2 NKJV

❦ A clear conscience is one of the many rewards you earn when you obey God's Word and follow His will. Whenever you know that you've done the right thing, you feel better about yourself, your life, and your future. A guilty conscience, on the other hand, is, for most people, it's own punishment.

In order to keep your conscience clear, you should study God's Word and obey it—you should seek God's will and follow it—you should honor God's Son and walk with Him. When you do, your earthly rewards are never-ceasing, and your heavenly rewards are everlasting.

❦ *One of the ways God has revealed Himself to us is in the conscience. Conscience is God's lamp within the human breast.*

Billy Graham

❦ *Christian joy is a gift from God flowing from a good conscience.*

St. Philip Neri

CARING FOR THE DOWNTRODDEN

*I tell you the truth, anything you did for even
the least of my people here, you also did for me.*

Matthew 25:40 NCV

❋ How fortunate we are to live in a land of opportunities and possibilities. But, for many people around the world, opportunities are scarce at best. In too many corners of the globe, hardworking men and women struggle mightily to provide food and shelter for their families.

When we care for the downtrodden, we follow in the footsteps of Christ. And, when we show compassion for those who suffer, we abide by the commandments of the One who created us. May we, who have been given so much, hear the Word of God . . . and may we follow it.

❋ *If you want to be truly happy, you won't find it on an endless quest for more stuff. You'll find it in receiving God's generosity and the passing that generosity along.*

Bill Hybels

❋ *A cup that is already full cannot have more added to it. In order to receive the further good to which we are entitled, we must give of that which we have.*

Margaret Becker

MOVING ON

*You have heard that it was said, "Love your neighbor and
hate your enemies." But I say to you, love your enemies.
Pray for those who hurt you.*

Matthew 5:43–44 NCV

❧ In Luke 6:37, Jesus instructs, "Judge not, and you
shall not be judged. Condemn not, and you shall not
be condemned. Forgive, and you will be forgiven."
(NKJV) Sometimes, people can be discourteous and
cruel. Sometimes people can be unfair, unkind, and
unappreciative. Sometimes people become angry and
frustrated. So what's a Christian to do? God's answer
is straightforward: forgive, forget, and move on.

Today and every day, make sure that you're quick
to forgive others for their shortcomings. And when
other people misbehave (as they most certainly will
from time to time), don't pay too much attention.
Just forgive those people as quickly as you can, and
try to move on . . . as quickly as you can.

❧ *A keen sense of humor helps us to overlook the
unbecoming, understand the unconventional, tolerate
the unpleasant, overcome the unexpected, and outlast the
unbearable.*

Billy Graham

THE SON OF ENCOURAGEMENT

Good people's words will help many others.

Proverbs 10:21 NCV

❧ Barnabas, a man whose name meant "Son of Encouragement," was a leader in the early Christian church. He was known for his kindness and for his ability to encourage others. Because of Barnabas, many people were introduced to Christ. And today, as believers living in a difficult world, we must seek to imitate the "Son of Encouragement."

We imitate Barnabas when we speak kind words to our families and to our friends. We imitate Barnabas when our actions give credence to our beliefs. We imitate Barnabas when we are generous with our possessions and with our praise. We imitate Barnabas when we give hope to the hopeless and encouragement to the downtrodden.

Today, be like Barnabas: become a source of encouragement to those who cross your path. When you do so, you will quite literally change the world, one person—and one moment—at a time.

❧ *God is still in the process of dispensing gifts, and He uses ordinary individuals like us to develop those gifts in other people.*

Howard Hendricks

YOUR ATTITUDE TODAY

Happiness makes a person smile,
but sadness can break a person's spirit.

Proverbs 15:13 NCV

❋ What is your attitude today? Are you fearful or worried? Are you more concerned about pleasing your friends than about pleasing your God? Are you bitter, confused, cynical or pessimistic? If so, it's time to have a little chat with your Father in heaven.

God intends that your life be filled with spiritual abundance and joy—but God will not force His joy upon you—you must choose it for yourself. So do yourself this favor: accept God's gifts with a smile on your face, a song on your lips, and joy in your heart. Think optimistically about yourself and your future. Give thanks to the One who has given you everything, and trust in your heart that He wants to give you so much more.

❋ *I may not be able to change the world I see around me, but I can change the way I see the world within me.*

John Maxwell

❋ *I became aware of one very important concept I had missed before: my attitude—not my circumstances—was what was making me unhappy.*

Vonette Bright

CARING FOR YOUR FAMILY

Whoever does not care for his own relatives, especially his own family members, has turned against the faith and is worse than someone who does not believe in God.

1 Timothy 5:8 NCV

❀ Despite the inevitable challenges of providing for your family, and despite the occasional hurt feelings of family life, your clan is God's gift to you. If God has blessed us with families, then He expects us to care for them. Sometimes, this profound responsibility seems daunting. And sometimes, even for the most dedicated Christians, family life holds moments of frustration and disappointment. But, for those who are lucky enough to live in the presence of a close-knit, caring clan, the rewards far outweigh the demands.

No family is perfect, and neither is yours. Give thanks to the Giver for the gift of family . . . and act accordingly.

❀ *When God asks someone to do something for Him entailing sacrifice, he makes up for it in surprising ways. Though He has led Bill all over the world to preach the gospel, He has not forgotten the little family in the mountains of North Carolina.*

Ruth Bell Graham

❀ *God expresses His love by putting us in a family.*

Charles Stanley

FRIENDSHIPS THAT HONOR GOD

*Blessed is the man who walks not in the counsel of
the ungodly, nor stands in the path of sinners,
nor sits in the seat of the scornful . . . .*

Psalm 1:1 NKJV

❧ Because we tend to become like our friends, we
must choose our friends carefully. Because our friends
influence us in ways that are both subtle and powerful,
we must ensure that our friendships are pleasing to
God. Some friendships help us honor God; these
friendships should be nurtured. Other friendships
place us in situations where we are tempted to
dishonor God by disobeying His commandments;
friendships such as these have the potential to do us
great harm.

When we spend our days in the presence of godly
believers, we are blessed, not only by those friends,
but also by our Creator.

❧ *Friends are like a quilt with lots of different shapes, sizes,
colors, and patterns of fabric. But the end result brings
you warmth and comfort in a support system that makes
your life richer and fuller.*

Suzanne Dale Ezell

❧ *I have found that the closer I am to the godly people
around me, the easier it is for me to live a righteous life
because they hold me accountable.*

John MacArthur

PROBLEMS IN PERSPECTIVE

*In my trouble I called to the Lord; I cried out
to my God. From his temple he heard my voice;
my call for help reached his ears.*

2 Samuel 22:7 NCV

❧ If a temporary loss has left you worried, exhausted, or both, it's time to readjust your thought patterns. Negative thoughts are habit-forming; thankfully, so are positive ones. With practice, you can form the habit of focusing on God's priorities and your possibilities. When you do, you'll soon discover that you will spend less time fretting about your challenges and more time praising God for His gifts.

When you call upon the Lord and prayerfully seek His will, He will give you wisdom and perspective. When you make God's priorities your priorities, He will direct your steps and calm your fears. So today and every day hereafter, pray for a sense of balance and perspective. And remember: no problems are too big for God—and that includes yours.

❧ *The Bible is a remarkable commentary on perspective. Through its divine message, we are brought face to face with issues and tests in daily living and how, by the power of the Holy Spirit, we are enabled to respond positively to them.*

Luci Swindoll

HOPE FOR THE JOURNEY

So we may boldly say: "The Lord is my helper;
I will not fear. What can man do to me?"

Hebrews 13:6 NKJV

❧ Circumstances should never dictate our attitudes toward life. Because we are saved by a risen Christ, we can have hope for the future, no matter how desperate our circumstances may seem. After all, God has promised that we are His throughout eternity. And, He has told us that we must place our hopes in Him.

Today, summon the courage to follow God. Even if the path seems difficult, even if your heart is fearful, trust your Heavenly Father and follow Him. Trust Him with your day and your life. Do His work, care for His children, and share His Good News. Let Him guide your steps. He will not lead you astray.

❧ *God knows that the strength that comes from wrestling with our fear will give us wings to fly.*

Paula Rinehart

❧ *Why rely on yourself and fall? Cast yourself upon His arm. Be not afraid. He will not let you slip. Cast yourself in confidence. He will receive you and heal you.*

St. Augustine

OBEY AND BE BLESSED

Now by this we know that we know Him,
if we keep His commandments.

1 John 2:3 NKJV

❋ We live in a world that presents us with countless temptations to stray far from God's path. Thus, God gave us His commandments so that we might obey them and be blessed. Oswald Chambers, the author of the Christian classic devotional text, *My Utmost For His Highest*, advised, "Never support an experience which does not have God as its source, and faith in God as its result." These words serve as a powerful reminder that, as Christians, we are called to walk with God and obey His commandments. We Christians, when confronted with sin, have clear instructions: Walk—or better yet run—in the opposite direction.

❋ *To yield to God means to belong to God, and to belong to God means to have all His infinite power. To belong to God means to have all.*

Hannah Whitall Smith

❋ *What our Lord said about cross-bearing and obedience is not in fine type. It is in bold print on the face of the contract.*

Vance Havner

THE ULTIMATE PROTECTION

The Lord himself will go before you.
He will be with you; he will not leave you or forget you.
Don't be afraid and don't worry.

Deuteronomy 31:8 NCV

❧ God has promised to protect us, and He intends to fulfill His promise. In a world filled with dangers and temptations, God is the ultimate armor. In a world filled with misleading messages, God's Word is the ultimate truth. In a world filled with more frustrations than we can count, God's Son offers the ultimate peace.

Will you accept God's peace and wear God's armor against the dangers of our world? Hopefully so, because when you do, you can live courageously, knowing that you possess the ultimate protection: God's unfailing love for you.

❧ *Our future may look fearfully intimidating, yet we can look up to the Engineer of the Universe, confident that nothing escapes His attention or slips out of the control of those strong hands.*

Elisabeth Elliot

❧ *Kept by His power—that is the only safety.*

Oswald Chambers

COUNTING YOUR BLESSINGS

Surely the righteous shall give thanks to Your name;
The upright shall dwell in Your presence.

Psalms 140:13 NKJV

※ Do you pay careful attention to the quality of your thoughts? And are you careful to direct those thoughts toward topics that are uplifting, enlightening, and pleasing to God? If so, congratulations. But if you find that your thoughts are hijacked from time to time by the negativity that seems to have invaded our troubled world, you are not alone. Ours is a society that focuses on—and often glamorizes—the negative aspects of life, and that's unfortunate.

God intends that you experience joy and abundance. So, today and every day hereafter, celebrate the life that God has given you by focusing your thoughts upon those things that are worthy of praise (Philippians 4:8). And while you're at it, count your blessings instead of your hardships. When you do, you'll undoubtedly offer words of thanks to your Heavenly Father for gifts that are simply too numerous to count.

※ *The Reference Point for the Christian is the Bible. All values, judgments, and attitudes must be gauged in relationship to this Reference Point.*

Ruth Bell Graham

COMMISSIONED TO SHARE THE GOOD NEWS

"Go therefore and make disciples of all the nations, baptizing them in the name of the Father and of the Son and of the Holy Spirit, teaching them to observe all things that I have commanded you; and lo, I am with you always, even to the end of the age." Amen.

Matthew 28:19-20 NKJV

❧ After His resurrection, Jesus addressed His disciples. As recorded in the 28th chapter of Matthew, Christ instructed His followers to share His message with the world. This "Great Commission" applies to Christians of every generation, including our own.

As believers, we are called to share the Good News of Jesus with our families, with our neighbors, and with the world. Christ commanded His disciples to become fishers of men. We must do likewise, and we must do so today. Tomorrow may indeed be too late.

❧ *Our commission is quite specific. We are told to be His witness to all nations. For us, as His disciples, to refuse any part of this commission frustrates the love of Jesus Christ, the Son of God.*

Catherine Marshall

HONORING GOD

*Honor the Lord with your wealth and the firstfruits
from all your crops. Then your barns will be full,
and your wine barrels will overflow with new wine.*

Proverbs 3:9-10 NCV

❊ When you honor God and place Him at the center
of your life, every day is a cause for celebration. But if
you fail to honor your Heavenly Father, you're asking
for trouble, and lots of it.

At times, your life is probably hectic, demanding,
and complicated. When the demands of life leave you
rushing from place to place with hardly a minute to
spare, you may fail to pause and thank your Creator
for the blessings He has bestowed upon you. But
that's a big mistake. So honor God for who He is and
for what He has done for you. And don't just honor
Him on Sunday morning. Praise Him all day long,
every day, for as long as you live . . . and then for all
eternity.

❊ *God shows unbridled delight when He sees people acting
in ways that honor Him.*

Bill Hybels

❊ *This is my story, this is my song, praising my Savior, all
the day long.*

Fanny Crosby

LET THE CELEBRATION BEGIN

*These things I have spoken to you, that My joy may
remain in you, and that your joy may be full.*

John 15:11 NKJV

❧ St. Augustine wrote: "The Christian ought to be
alleluia from head to foot." Oswald Chambers echoed
that thought when he wrote, "Joy is the great note all
throughout the Bible." But, even the most dedicated
Christians can, on occasion, forget to celebrate each
day for what it is: a priceless gift from God.

Today, let us be joyful Christians with smiles on
our faces and kind words on our lips. After all, this is
God's day, and He has given us clear instructions for
its use. We are commanded to rejoice and be glad. So,
with no further ado, let the celebration begin...

❧ *Joy can be the echo of God's life within you.*

Duane Pederson

❧ *It is the definition of joy to be able to offer back to God
the essence of what he's placed in you, be that creativity
or a love of ideas or a compassionate heart or the gift of
hospitality.*

Paula Rinehart

❧ *Joy is the simplest form of gratitude.*

Karl Barth

FALLING IN LOVE . . . WITH GOD

You shall love the Lord your God with all your heart,
with all your soul, and with all your strength.

Deuteronomy 6:5 NKJV

❋ Vance Havner observed, "The church has no greater need than to fall in love with Jesus all over again." How true. When churches (and their members!) fall in love with God and His only begotten Son, great things happen.

When we worship God faithfully and obediently, we invite His love into our hearts. When we truly love God, we allow Him to rule over our days and our lives. In turn, we grow to love God even more deeply as we sense His love for us.

Today, open your heart to the Father and to the Son. And let your obedience be a fitting response to their never-ending love.

❋ *When we develop an authentic love relationship with God, we will not be able to keep Him compartmentalized in "churchy," religious categories.*

Beth Moore

❋ *When our heart's desire is to please our Lord because we love Him, there will be no time for second thoughts or second opinions.*

Warren Wiersbe

THE WISDOM TO OBEY

And the world is passing away, and the lust of it;
but he who does the will of God abides forever.

1 John 2:17 NKJV

❋ God has given us a guidebook for righteous living called the Holy Bible. It contains thorough instructions which, if followed, lead to fulfillment, righteousness and salvation. But, if we choose to ignore God's commandments, the results are as predictable as they are tragic. Since God created Adam and Eve, we human beings have been rebelling against our Creator. Why? Because we are unwilling to trust God's Word, and we are unwilling to follow His commandments.

Talking about God is easy; living by His commandments is considerably harder. But, unless we are willing to abide by God's laws, all of our righteous proclamations ring hollow. How can we best proclaim our love for the Lord? By obeying Him. And, for further instructions, read the manual.

❋ *Happiness is obedience, and obedience is happiness.*

C. H. Spurgeon

❋ *God does not want the forced obedience of slaves. Instead, He covets the voluntary love and obedience of children who love Him for Himself.*

Catherine Marshall

THE CHAINS OF PERFECTIONISM

Those who wait for perfect weather will never plant seeds; those who look at every cloud will never harvest crops.

Ecclesiastes 11:4 NCV

❋ The media delivers an endless stream of messages that tell you how to look, how to behave, and how to dress. The media's expectations are impossible to meet—God's are not. God doesn't expect perfection . . . and neither should you.

If you find yourself bound up by the chains of perfectionism, it's time to ask yourself who you're trying to impress, and why. If you're trying to impress other people, it's time to reconsider your priorities. Your first responsibility is to the Heavenly Father who created you and to His Son who saved you. But, when it comes to meeting society's unrealistic expectations, forget it! After all, pleasing God is simply a matter of obeying His commandments and accepting His Son. But as for pleasing everybody else? That's impossible!

❋ *Nothing would be done at all, if a man waited until he could do it so well that no one could find fault with it.*

John Henry Cardinal Newman

❋ *Excellence is not perfection, but essentially a desire to be strong in the Lord and for the Lord.*

Cynthia Heald

A SERIES OF CHOICES

*The thing you should want most is God's kingdom
and doing what God wants. Then all these other things
you need will be given to you.*

Matthew 6:33 NCV

❋ As a believer who has been transformed by the love of Jesus, you have every reason to make wise choices. But sometimes, when the daily grind threatens to grind you up and spit you out, you may make choices that are displeasing to God. When you do, you'll pay a price because you'll forfeit the happiness and the peace that might otherwise have been yours.

So, as you pause to consider the kind of Christian you are—and the kind of Christian you want to become—ask yourself whether you're sitting on the fence or standing in the light. The choice is yours . . . and so are the consequences.

❋ *Many jokes are made about the devil, but the devil is no joke. He is called a deceiver. In order to accomplish his purpose, the devil blinds people to their need for Christ. Two forces are at work in our world—the forces of Christ and the forces of the devil—and you are asked to choose.*

Billy Graham

❋ *No matter how many books you read, no matter how many schools you attend, you're never really wise until you start making wise choices.*

Marie T. Freeman

THE SOURCE OF ALL COMFORT

I was very worried, but you comforted me . . . .

Psalm 94:19 NCV

❋ We are wise to remember the words of Jesus, who, when He walked on the waters, reassured His disciples, saying, "Take courage! It is I. Don't be afraid" (Matthew 14:27 NIV). Then, with Christ on His throne—and with trusted friends and loving family members at our sides—we can face our fears with courage and with faith.

Are you facing a difficult challenge? If so, remember the ultimate Source of your comfort . . . and start talking to Him right now.

❋ *When I am criticized, injured, or afraid, there is a Father who is ready to comfort me.*

Max Lucado

❋ *No journey is complete that does not lead through some dark valleys. We can properly comfort others only with the comfort we ourselves have been given by God.*

Vance Havner

❋ *He is always thinking about us. We are before his eyes. The Lord's eye never sleeps, but is always watching out for our welfare. We are continually on his heart.*

C. H. Spurgeon

HE RENEWS OUR STRENGTH

Anxiety in the heart of man causes depression,
but a good word makes it glad.

Proverbs 12:25 NKJV

❖ When we fail to meet the expectations of others (or, for that matter, the expectations that we have set for ourselves), we may be tempted to abandon hope. Thankfully, on those cloudy days when our strength is sapped and our faith is shaken, there exists a source from which we can draw courage and wisdom. That source is God.

When we seek to form a more intimate and dynamic relationship with our Creator, He renews our spirits and restores our souls. God's promise is made clear in Ezekiel 36:26, "I will give you a new heart and put a new spirit within you." (NKJV) And upon this promise we can—and should—depend.

❖ *Don't let aridity distress you: perfection has nothing to do with such things—only with virtues. Your devotion will come back when you are least expecting it.*

St. Teresa of Avila

❖ *The same God who empowered Samson, Gideon, and Paul seeks to empower my life and your life, because God hasn't changed.*

Bill Hybels

STRENGTH FOR ANY CHALLENGE

*I have carried you since you were born; I have taken
care of you from your birth. Even when you are old,
I will be the same. Even when your hair has turned gray,
I will take care of you. I made you and will
take care of you. I will carry you and save you.*

Isaiah 46:3-4 NCV

❧ God's love and support never changes. From the
cradle to the grave, God has promised to give you the
strength to meet any challenge. God has promised to
lift you up and guide your steps if you let Him. God
has promised that when you entrust your life to Him
completely and without reservation, He will give you
the courage to face any trial and the wisdom to live in
His righteousness.

God's hand uplifts those who turn their hearts and
prayers to Him. Will you count yourself among that
number? Will you accept God's peace and wear God's
armor against the temptations and distractions of our
dangerous world? If you do, you can live courageously
and optimistically, knowing that you have been
forever touched by the loving, unfailing, uplifting
hand of God.

❧ *He can accomplish anything He chooses to do. If He
ever asks you to do something, He Himself will enable
you to do it.*

Henry Blackaby

ABOUT TIME

So teach us to number our days,
that we may gain a heart of wisdom.

Psalm 90:12 NKJV

❧ Time is a nonrenewable gift from God. But sometimes, we treat our time here on earth as if it were not a gift at all: We may be tempted to invest our lives in trivial pursuits and petty diversions. But our Father beckons each of us to a higher calling.

An important element of our stewardship to God is the way that we choose to spend the time He has entrusted to us. Each waking moment holds the potential to do a good deed, to say a kind word, or to offer a heartfelt prayer. Our challenge, as believers, is use our time wisely in the service of God's work and in accordance with His plan for our lives.

Each day is a special treasure to be savored and celebrated. May we—as Christians who have so much to celebrate—never fail to praise our Creator by rejoicing in this glorious day, and by using it wisely.

❧ *Our leisure, even our play, is a matter of serious concern. There is no neutral ground in the universe: every square inch, every split second, is claimed by God and counterclaimed by Satan.*

C. S. Lewis

SERENITY NOW

Forget what happened before, and do not think about
the past. Look at the new thing I am going to do.
It is already happening. Don't you see it? I will make
a road in the desert and rivers in the dry land.

Isaiah 43:18-19 NCV

If you've encountered unfortunate circumstances that are beyond your power to control, accept those circumstances . . . and trust God. The American Theologian Reinhold Niebuhr composed a profoundly simple verse that came to be known as the Serenity Prayer: "God, grant me the serenity to accept the things I cannot change, the courage to change the things I can, and the wisdom to know the difference." Niebuhr's words are far easier to recite than they are to live by. Why? Because most of us want life to unfold in accordance with to our own wishes and timetables. But sometimes God has other plans.

When you trust God, you can be comforted in the knowledge that your Creator is both loving and wise, and that He understands His plans perfectly, even when you do not.

Acceptance is taking from God's hand absolutely anything He gives, looking into His face in trust and thanksgiving, knowing that the confinement of the situation we're in is good and for His glory.

Charles Swindoll

OUR ROCK IN TURBULENT TIMES

*And he said: "The Lord is my rock and my fortress
and my deliverer; the God of my strength,
in whom I will trust."*

2 Samuel 22:2-3 NKJV

➣ As believers, we know that God loves us and that He will protect us. In times of hardship, God offers to comfort us; in times of sorrow, He offers to dry our tears. The words of Jesus offer us comfort: "These things I have spoken to you, that in Me you may have peace. In the world you will have tribulation; but be of good cheer, I have overcome the world" (John 16: 33 NKJV).

When we are troubled, or weak, or sorrowful, God is always with us. We must build our lives on the rock that cannot be shaken: we must trust in God. And then, we must get on with the hard work of tackling our problems . . . because if we don't, who will? Or should?

➣ *The Rock of Ages is the great sheltering encirclement.*

Oswald Chambers

➣ *We all go through pain and sorrow, but the presence of God, like a warm, comforting blanket, can shield us and protect us, and allow the deep inner joy to surface, even in the most devastating circumstances.*

Barbara Johnson

WHY BAD THINGS?

They won't be afraid of bad news;
their hearts are steady because they trust the Lord.

Psalm 112:7 NCV

❧ If God is good, and if He made the world, why do bad things happen? Part of that question is easy to answer, and part of it isn't. Let's get to the easy part first: Sometimes, bad things happen because people disobey God's commandments and invite sadness and heartache into God's beautiful world.

But on other occasions, bad things happen, and it's nobody's fault. So who is to blame? Sometimes, nobody is to blame. Sometimes, things just happen and we simply cannot know why. Thankfully, all our questions will be answered . . . some day. The Bible promises that in heaven we will understand all the reasons behind God's plans. But until then, we must simply trust that God is good, and that, in the end, He will make things right.

❧ *There is but one good; that is God. Everything else is good when it looks to Him and bad when it turns from Him.*

C. S. Lewis

❧ *On the darkest day of your life, God is still in charge. Take comfort in that.*

Marie T. Freeman

QUICKSAND

Let all bitterness, wrath, anger, clamor, and evil speaking
be put away from you, with all malice.
And be kind to one another, tenderhearted,
forgiving one another, just as God in Christ forgave you.

Ephesians 4:31-32 NKJV

Are you mired in the quicksand of bitterness or regret? If so, you are not only disobeying God's Word, you are also wasting your time.

The world holds few if any rewards for those who remain angrily focused upon the past. Still, the act of forgiveness is difficult for all but the most saintly men and women.

Being frail, fallible, imperfect human beings, most of us are quick to anger, quick to blame, slow to forgive, and even slower to forget. Yet as Christians, we are commanded to forgive others, just as we, too, have been forgiven.

If there exists even one person—alive or dead—against whom you hold bitter feelings, it's time to forgive. Or, if you are embittered against yourself for some past mistake or shortcoming, it's finally time to forgive yourself and move on. Hatred, bitterness, and regret are not part of God's plan for your life. Forgiveness is.

Bitterness is the trap that snares the hunter.

Max Lucado

WHAT DOESN'T CHANGE

Jesus Christ is the same yesterday, today, and forever.
Hebrews 13:8 NCV

☙ Some things change and some things do not. Our world is in constant flux. Our God is the same yesterday, today, and tomorrow.

At times, the world seems to be trembling beneath our feet. But we can be comforted in the knowledge that our Heavenly Father is the rock that cannot be shaken. His Word promises, "I am the Lord, I do not change" (Malachi 3:6 NKJV).

Every day that we live, we mortals encounter a multitude of changes—some good, some not so good, some downright disheartening. On those occasions when us must endure life-changing personal losses that leave us breathless, there is a place we can turn for comfort and assurance—we can turn to God. When we do, our loving Heavenly Father stands ready to protect us, to comfort us, to guide us, and, in time, to heal us.

☙ *In a world kept chaotic by change, you will eventually discover, as I have, that this is one of the most precious qualities of the God we are looking for: He doesn't change.*

Bill Hybels

OUR CHILDREN, OUR HOPE

But when Jesus saw it, He was greatly displeased and said to them, "Let the little children come to Me, and do not forbid them; for of such is the kingdom of God."

Mark 10:14 NKJV

⮞ Children come in different shapes and sizes, and personalities and temperaments. But one common denominator remains: each child is a priceless gift from God. And, with God's gift comes immense responsibilities.

Our children are our nation's most precious resource. And, as responsible parents, we must create homes in which the future generation can grow and flourish.

Today, let us pray for our children . . . all of them. Let us pray for children here at home and for children around the world. Every child is God's child. May we, as concerned adults, behave—and pray—accordingly.

⮞ *Let us look upon our children; let us love them and train them as children of the covenant and children of the promise. These are the children of God.*

Andrew Murray

⮞ *Every child born into the world is a new thought of God, an ever-fresh and radiant possibility.*

Kate Douglas Wiggin

CONFIDENT CHRISTIANITY

You are my hope, O Lord God;
You are my trust from my youth.

Psalm 71:5 NKJV

☙ We live in a world that fosters insecurity and doubts. But because we are Christians, we have many reasons to be confident. God loves us; Christ has saved us, and we have far more blessings than we can count. Yet sometimes, even the most devout believers can become discouraged. Discouragement, however, is not God's way; He is a God of possibility, not negativity.

Are you a confident Christian? You should be. God's grace is eternal and His promises are unambiguous. So count your blessings, not your hardships. And live courageously. God is the Giver of all things good, and He watches over you today and forever.

☙ *If our minds are stayed upon God, His peace will rule the affairs entertained by our minds. If, on the other hand, we allow our minds to dwell on the cares of this world, God's peace will be far from our thoughts.*

Woodroll Kroll

☙ *There is no other method of living piously and justly than that of depending upon God.*

John Calvin

His Promises

Let us hold fast the confession of our hope without wavering, for He who promised is faithful.

Hebrews 10:23 NKJV

❧ The Christian faith is founded upon promises that are contained in a unique book. That book is the Holy Bible. The Bible is a roadmap for life here on earth and for life eternal. As Christians, we are called upon to study its meaning, to trust its promises, to follow its commandments, and to share its Good News. God's Holy Word is, indeed, a transforming, life-changing book, and a passing acquaintance with the Good News is insufficient for Christians who seek to obey God's Word and understand His will.

God has made promises to you, and He intends to keep them. So take God at His word: trust His promises and share them with your family, with your friends, and with the world.

❧ *We can have full confidence in God's promises because we can have full faith in His character.*

Franklin Graham

❧ *The promises of God's Word sustain us in our suffering, and we know Jesus sympathizes and empathizes with us in our darkest hour.*

Bill Bright

MOUNTAINTOPS AND VALLEYS

I sought the Lord, and He heard me,
and delivered me from all my fears.

Psalm 34:4 NKJV

When you reach the mountaintops of life, praising God is easy. But, when the storm clouds form overhead, your faith will be tested, sometimes to the breaking point. Every life (including yours) is an unfolding series of events: some fabulous, some not-so-fabulous, and some downright disheartening. As a believer, you can take comfort in this fact: Wherever you find yourself, whether at the top of the mountain or the depths of the valley, God is there, and because He cares for you, you can live courageously.

The next time you find your courage tested to the limit, remember that God is your shield and your strength; He is your protector and your deliverer. Call upon Him in your hour of need and He will protect you.

How can God direct our steps if we're not taking any?

Sarah Leah Grafstein

There comes a time when we simply have to face the challenges in our lives and stop backing down.

John Eldredge

DEALING WITH DISAPPOINTMENT

*For we do not want you to be ignorant, brethren,
of our trouble which came to us in Asia: that we were
burdened beyond measure, above strength, so that
we despaired even of life. Yes, we had the sentence
of death in ourselves, that we should not trust in
ourselves but in God who raises the dead,
who delivered us from so great a death, and does
deliver us; in whom we trust that He will still deliver us.*

2 Corinthians 1:8-10 NKJV

From time to time, all of us face life-altering disappointments that leave us breathless. Oftentimes, these disappointments come unexpectedly, leaving us with more questions than answers. But even when we don't have all the answers—or, for that matter, even when we don't seem to have any of the answers—God does. Whatever our circumstances, whether we stand atop the highest mountain or wander through the darkest valley, God is ready to protect us, to comfort us, and to heal us. Our task is to let Him.

The next time you're disappointed, don't panic and don't give up. Just be patient and let God remind you he's still in control.

Max Lucado

PATS ON THE BACK

*So let us try to do what makes peace
and helps one another.*

Romans 14:19 NCV

☙ In the book of Ephesians, Paul writes, "When you talk, do not say harmful things, but say what people need—words that will help others become stronger. Then what you say will do good to those who listen to you." (4:29 NCV). Paul reminds us that when we choose our words carefully, we can have a powerful impact on those around us.

Life is a team sport, and all of us need occasional pats on the back from our teammates.

Since we don't always know which people need our help the most, the best strategy is to encourage all the people who cross our paths. So today, be a world-class source of encouragement to everyone you meet. Never has the need been greater.

☙ *Make it a rule, and pray to God to help you to keep it, never to lie down at night without being able to say: "I have made at least one human being a little wiser, a little happier, or a little better this day."*

Charles Kingsley

☙ *Keep your fears to yourself, but share your courage with others.*

Robert Louis Stevenson

THE ATTITUDE OF A LEADER

The wise people will shine like the brightness of the sky.
Those who teach others to live right will shine
like stars forever and ever.

Daniel 12:3 NCV

❧ If you are in a position of leadership, whether as a parent, or as a leader at your work, your church, or your school, it's up to you to set the right tone by maintaining the right attitude. John Maxwell writes, "Great leaders understand that the right attitude will set the right atmosphere, which enables the right response from others."

Our world needs Christian leaders, and so do your family members and coworkers. You can become a trusted, competent, thoughtful leader if you learn to maintain the right attitude: one that is realistic, optimistic, forward looking, and Christ-centered.

❧ *A Christian leader will succeed if she convinces her followers that God—as well as she herself—recognizes and honors the person's strengths and abilities, and that each worker has something of value to offer others.*

Linda McGinn

❧ *When God wants to accomplish something, He calls dedicated men and women to challenge His people and lead the way.*

Warren Wiersbe

FAITH TO SHARE

That is why I was chosen to tell the Good News and to be an apostle. (I am telling the truth; I am not lying.) I was chosen to teach those who are not Jews to believe and to know the truth.

1 Timothy 2:7 NCV

If heaven is such a wonderful place (and it is!), why doesn't God simply take us there when we become believers? The answer is simple: We still have work to do. And an important part of that work involves our faith—building it and sharing it.

When a suffering woman sought healing by merely touching the hem of His cloak, Jesus replied, "Daughter, be of good comfort; thy faith hath made thee whole" (Matthew 9:22 KJV). The message to believers of every generation is clear: we must live by faith today and every day.

How can you strengthen your faith? Through praise, through worship, through Bible study, and through prayer. And, as your faith becomes stronger, you will find ways to share it with your friends, your family, and with the world . . . and that, by the way, is exactly what God wants you to do.

Our faith grows by expression. If we want to keep our faith, we must share it. We must act.

Billy Graham

THE CORNERSTONE

*Let us run with endurance the race that is set before us,
looking unto Jesus, the author and finisher of our faith,
who for the joy that was set before Him endured
the cross, despising the shame, and has sat down at
the right hand of the throne of God.*

Hebrews 12:1-2 NKJV

❧ God has given you the gift of eternal life through His Son. In response to God's priceless gift, you are instructed to focus your thoughts, your prayers, and your energies upon God and His only begotten Son.

Is Christ the focus of your life? Are you fired with enthusiasm for Him? Are you an energized Christian who allows God's Son to reign over every aspect of your day? Make no mistake: that's exactly what God intends for you to do.

To stay focused on Christ, you must resist the subtle yet powerful temptation to become a "spiritual dabbler." A person who dabbles in the Christian faith is unwilling to place God above all other things. Resist that temptation; make God the cornerstone and the touchstone of your life. When you do, He will give you all the strength and wisdom you need to live victoriously for Him.

❧ *Give me the person who says, "This one thing I do, and not these fifty things I dabble in."*

D. L. Moody

FORGIVENESS AND FREEDOM

And forgive us our sins, for we ourselves also forgive everyone in debt to us.

Luke 11:4 NKJV

As a believer who is the recipient of God's forgiveness, how should you behave towards others? Should you forgive them (just as God has forgiven you) or should you remain embittered and resentful?

God's power to forgive, like His love, is infinite. Despite your shortcomings, despite your sins, God offers you immediate forgiveness and eternal life when you accept Christ as your Savior.

God's Word instructs you to forgive others. When you do, you not only obey God's command, you also free yourself from a prison of your own making . . . and that's a very nice thing to do for yourself.

The well of God's forgiveness never runs dry.

Grady Nutt

Forgiveness is actually the best revenge because it not only sets us free from the person we forgive, but it frees us to move into all that God has in store for us.

Stormie Omartian

SHARING THE JOY

Every day is hard for those who suffer,
but a happy heart is like a continual feast.

Proverbs 15:15 NCV

❧ Christ promises us lives of abundance and joy, but He does not force His joy upon us. We must claim His joy for ourselves, and when we do, Jesus, in turn, fills our spirits with His power and His love. Few things in life are more sad, or, for that matter, more absurd, than a grumpy Christian.

How can we receive from Christ the joy that is rightfully ours? By giving Him what is rightfully His: our hearts and our souls.

When we earnestly commit ourselves to the Savior of mankind, when we place Jesus at the center of our lives and trust Him as our personal Savior, He will transform us, not just for today, but for all eternity. Then we, as God's children, can share Christ's joy and His message with a world that needs both.

❧ *Sour godliness is the devil's religion.*

John Wesley

❧ *The greatest honor you can give Almighty God is to live gladly and joyfully because of the knowledge of His love.*

Juliana of Norwich

THE ULTIMATE INSTRUCTION MANUAL

He who despises the word will be destroyed,
But he who fears the commandment will be rewarded.

Proverbs 13:13 NKJV

❧ God's commandments are not suggestions. They are given by a loving God who wants the best for His children.

The Holy Bible contains thorough instructions which, if followed, lead to fulfillment, righteousness, and salvation. But, if we choose to ignore God's commandments, the results are as predictable as they are tragic.

A righteous life has many components: faith, honesty, generosity, love, kindness, humility, gratitude, and worship, to name but a few. If we seek to follow the steps of our Savior, Jesus Christ, we must seek to live according to His commandments. Let us follow God's commandments, and let us conduct our lives in such a way that we might be shining examples for those who have not yet found Christ.

❧ *Bible history is filled with people who began the race with great success but failed at the end because they disregarded God's rules.*

Warren Wiersbe

LIMITLESS POWER, LIMITLESS LOVE

*I pray also that you will have greater understanding
in your heart so you will know the hope to which he has
called us and that you will know how rich and glorious
are the blessings God has promised his holy people.
And you will know that God's power is
very great for us who believe.*

Ephesians 1:18-19 NCV

Because God's power is limitless, it is far beyond the comprehension of mortal minds. Even though we cannot fully understand the awesome power of God, we can praise it. When we worship God with faith and assurance, when we place Him at the absolute center of our lives, we invite His love into our hearts. In turn, we grow to love Him more deeply as we sense His love for us. St. Augustine wrote, "I love you, Lord, not doubtingly, but with absolute certainty. Your Word beat upon my heart until I fell in love with you, and now the universe and everything in it tells me to love you."

Let us pray that we, too, will turn our hearts to the Creator, knowing with certainty that His heart has ample room for each of us, and that we, in turn, must make room in our hearts for Him.

Think big, talk big, act big. Because we have a big God.

Kathryn Kuhlman

GOD'S TIMETABLE

Therefore humble yourselves under the mighty hand of God, that He may exalt you in due time.

1 Peter 5:6 NKJV

☙ Sometimes, the hardest thing to do is to wait. This is especially true when we're in a hurry and when we want things to happen now, if not sooner! But God's plan does not always happen in the way that we would like or at the time of our own choosing. Our task—as believing Christians who trust in a benevolent, all knowing Father—is to wait patiently for God to reveal Himself.

We human beings are, by nature, impatient. We know what we want, and we know exactly when we want it: RIGHT NOW! But, God knows better. He has created a world that unfolds according to His own timetable, not ours . . . thank goodness!

☙ *Events of all sorts creep or fly exactly as God pleases.*

William Cowper

☙ *Even Jesus, clear as he was about his calling, had to get his instructions one day at a time. One time he was told to wait, another time to go.*

Laurie Beth Jones

GROWING IN CHRIST

*When I was a child, I spoke as a child, I understood
as a child, I thought as a child; but when
I became a man, I put away childish things.*

1 Corinthians 13:11 NKJV

~ The journey toward spiritual maturity lasts a lifetime. As Christians, we can and should continue to grow in the love and the knowledge of our Savior as long as we live. Norman Vincent Peale had the following advice for believers of all ages: "Ask the God who made you to keep remaking you." That advice, of course, is perfectly sound, but often ignored.

When we cease to grow, either emotionally or spiritually, we do ourselves a profound disservice. But, if we study God's word, if we obey His commandments, and if we live in the center of His will, we will not be "stagnant" believers; we will, instead, be growing Christians . . . and that's exactly what God wants for our lives.

~ *No matter what we are going through, no matter how long the waiting for answers, of one thing we may be sure. God is faithful. He keeps His promises. What he starts, He finishes...including His perfect work in us.*

Gloria Gaither

WHEN HONESTY IS DIFFICULT

The honest person will live in safety,
but the dishonest will be caught.

Proverbs 10:9 NCV

Honesty is God's policy, and lasting relationships are built upon a foundation of honesty and trust. It has been said on many occasions that honesty is the best policy. We are to be servants worthy of our Savior, Jesus Christ, we must be honest and forthright in all our communications with others.

Sometimes, honesty is difficult; sometimes, honesty is painful; sometimes, honesty makes us feel uncomfortable. Despite these temporary feelings of discomfort, we must make honesty the hallmark of all our relationships; otherwise, we invite needless suffering into our own lives and into the lives of those we love.

The commandment of absolute truthfulness is really only another name for the fullness of discipleship.

Dietrich Bonhoeffer

The single most important element in any human relationship is honesty—with oneself, with God, and with others.

Catherine Marshall

HIS JOY . . . AND OURS

Rejoice in the Lord always. Again I will say, rejoice!

Philippians 4:4 NKJV

❧ Christ made it clear: He intends that His joy should become our joy. Yet sometimes, amid the inevitable hustle and bustle of life, we can forfeit—albeit temporarily—the joy of Christ as we wrestle with the challenges of daily living.

Billy Graham correctly observed, "When Jesus Christ is the source of our joy, no words can describe it." And C. S. Lewis noted that, "Joy is the serious business of heaven." So here's a prescription for better spiritual health: Open the door of your soul to Christ. When you do, He will give you His peace and His joy . . . and you'll be eternally grateful that He did.

❧ *When I think of God, my heart is so full of joy that the notes leap and dance as they leave my pen; and since God has given me a cheerful heart, I serve him with a cheerful spirit.*

Franz Joseph Haydn

❧ *As I contemplate all the sacrifices required in order to live a life that is totally focused on Jesus Christ and His eternal kingdom, the joy seeps out of my heart onto my face in a smile of deep satisfaction.*

Anne Graham Lotz

FAMILY PRIORITIES

Choose for yourselves this day whom you will serve . . .
But as for me and my house, we will serve the Lord.

Joshua 24:15 NKJV

☞ It takes time to build a strong family . . . lots of time. Yet we live in a world where time seems to be an ever-shrinking commodity as we rush from place to place with seldom a moment to spare.

Has the busy pace of life robbed you of sufficient time with your loved ones? If so, it's time to adjust your priorities. And God can help.

When you allow God to help you organize your day, you'll soon discover that there is ample time for your spouse, your children, your parents, and your siblings. So, as you plan for the day ahead, make God's priorities your priorities. When you do, every other priority will have a tendency to fall neatly into place.

☞ *Apart from religious influence, the family is the most important influence on society.*

Billy Graham

☞ *A man ought to live so that everybody knows he is a Christian, and most of all, his family ought to know.*

D. L. Moody

☞ *The family that prays together, stays together.*

Anonymous

BLESSED OBEDIENCE

Return to the Lord your God and obey His voice,
according to all that I command you today, you and
your children, with all your heart and with all your
soul, that the Lord your God will bring you back from
captivity, and have compassion on you.

Deuteronomy 30:2-3 NKJV

≈ Talking about God is easy; living by His laws is considerably harder. But unless we are willing to live obediently, all our righteous words ring hollow. We live in a world filled with temptations, distractions, and countless opportunities to disobey God. But as believers who seek to be godly examples for our families and friends, we must turn our thoughts and our hearts away from the evils of this world. We must turn instead to God.

How can we best proclaim our love for the Lord? By obeying Him. We must seek God's counsel and trust the counsel He gives. And, when we invite God into our hearts and live according to His commandments, we are blessed today, and tomorrow, and forever.

≈ *God is God. Because He is God, He is worthy of my trust and obedience. I will find rest nowhere but in His holy will, a will that is unspeakably beyond my largest notions of what He is up to.*

Elisabeth Elliot

By Perseverance . . .

But thanks be to God, who gives us the victory
through our Lord Jesus Christ. Therefore, my beloved
brethren, be steadfast, immovable, always abounding
in the work of the Lord, knowing that your labor
is not in vain in the Lord.

1 Corinthians 15:57-58 NKJV

❧ As you continue to seek God's purpose for your life, you will undoubtedly experience your fair share of disappointments, detours, false starts, and failures. When you do, don't become discouraged: God's not finished with you yet.

The old saying is as true today as it was when it was first spoken: "Life is a marathon, not a sprint." That's why wise travelers select a traveling companion who never tires and never falters. That partner, of course, is your Heavenly Father. So pray as if everything depended upon God, and work as if everything depended upon you. And trust God to do the rest.

❧ *Your life is not a boring stretch of highway. It's a straight line to heaven. And just look at the fields ripening along the way. Look at the tenacity and endurance. Look at the grains of righteousness. You'll have quite a crop at harvest...so don't give up!*

Joni Eareckson Tada

FOOLISH PRIDE

*When you do things, do not let selfishness or pride
be your guide. Instead, be humble and give more
honor to others than to yourselves.*

Philippians 2:3 NCV

❧ Most of us aspire for the "good life." We dream of days filled with happiness and laughter, and days with little want and need. But there is some danger in the "good life." Sometimes our faith is tested more by prosperity than by adversity. Why? Because in times of plenty, we are tempted to stick out our chests and say, "I did that." But nothing could be further from the truth. All of our blessings start and end with God, and whatever "it" is, He did it. And He deserves the credit.

Who are the greatest among us? Are they the proud and the powerful? Hardly. The greatest among us are the humble servants who care less for their own glory and more for God's glory. If we seek greatness in God's eyes, we must forever praise God's good works, not our own.

❧ *When we look at the individual parts of our lives, some things appear unfair and unpleasant. When we take them out of the context of the big picture, we easily drift into the attitude that we deserve better, and the tumble down into the pit of pride begins.*

Susan Hunt

SEEKING AND FINDING

*Ask, and God will give to you. Search, and you will
find. Knock, and the door will open for you.
Yes, everyone who asks will receive.
Everyone who searches will find. And everyone who
knocks will have the door opened.*

Matthew 7:7-8 NCV

➭ Where is God? God is eternally with us. He is
omnipresent. He is, quite literally, everywhere you
have ever been and everywhere you will ever go.
He is with you night and day; He knows your every
thought; He hears your every heartbeat.

Sometimes, in the crush of your daily duties,
God may seem far away. Or sometimes, when the
disappointments and sorrows of life leave you
brokenhearted, God may seem distant, but He is not.
When you earnestly seek God, you will find Him
because He is here, waiting patiently for you to reach
out to Him . . . right here . . . right now.

➭ *Our souls were made to live in an upper atmosphere,
and we stifle and choke if we live on any lower level. Our
eyes were made to look off from these heavenly heights,
and our vision is distorted by any lower gazing.*

Hannah Whitall Smith

LOOK UP

*Set your mind on things above,
not on things on the earth.*

Colossians 3:2 NKJV

~ Thoughts are intensely powerful things. Our thoughts have the power to lift us up or drag us down; they have the power to energize us or deplete us, to inspire us to greater accomplishments or to make those accomplishments impossible.

Bishop Fulton Sheen correctly observed, "The mind is like a clock that is constantly running down. It needs to be wound up daily with good thoughts." But sometimes, even for the most faithful believers, winding up our intellectual clocks is difficult indeed.

If negative thoughts have left you worried, exhausted, or both, it's time to readjust your thought patterns. Negative thinking is habit-forming; thankfully, so is positive thinking. And it's up to you to train your mind to focus on God's power and your possibilities. Both are far greater than you can imagine.

~ *The things we think are the things that feed our souls. If we think on pure and lovely things, we shall grow pure and lovely like them; and the converse is equally true.*

Hannah Whitall Smith

THE TREASURE HUNT

Do not love the world or the things in the world.
If you love the world, the love of the Father is not in you.
1 John 2:15 NCV

❧ All of mankind is engaged in a colossal, worldwide treasure hunt. Many people seek treasure from earthly sources, treasures such as material wealth or public acclaim. But the smart and successful ones seek God's treasures by making Him the cornerstone of their lives.

What kind of treasure hunter are you? Are you so caught up in the demands of everyday living that you sometimes allow the search for worldly treasures to become your primary focus? If so, it's time to reorganize your daily to-do list by placing God in His rightful place: first place. Don't allow anyone or anything to separate you from your Heavenly Father and His only begotten Son.

The world's treasures are difficult to find and difficult to keep; God's treasures are ever-present and everlasting. Which treasures, then, will you claim as your own?

❧ *Nothing is more foolish than a security built upon the world and its promises, for they are all vanity and a lie.*
Matthew Henry

❧ *Why is love of gold more potent than love of souls?*
Lottie Moon

TOTAL TRUST

Trust in Him at all times, you people; pour out your heart before Him; God is a refuge for us.

Psalm 62:8 NKJV

On the sunnier days of life, we find it easy to praise God, to trust Him, and to give thanks. But, when we endure the storms of bitterness and despair, trusting God is more difficult.

The next time you find your courage tested to the limit, lean upon God's promises. Trust His Son. When you are worried, anxious, or afraid, call upon Him. God can manage your troubles infinitely better than you can, so turn them over to Him. Remember that God rules both the sunny days and the darker ones—with limitless wisdom and love—now and forever.

I'm discovering that the first step toward a vital, trusting relationship with God is speaking the truth— bringing myself out of the shadows and talking honestly to my Father.

Sheila Walsh

Trusting God completely means having faith that he knows what is best for your life. You expect him to keep his promises, help you with problems, and do the impossible when necessary.

Rick Warren

ABUNDANCE AND PEACE

The peace of God, which surpasses all understanding,
will guard your hearts and minds through Christ Jesus.

Philippians 4:7 NKJV

∞ If you are a thoughtful believer, you will open yourself to the spiritual abundance that your Savior offers by following Him completely and without reservation. When you do, you will receive the love, the peace, and the joy that He has promised.

Do you sincerely seek the riches that our Savior offers to those who give themselves to Him? Then follow Him. When you do, you will receive the love and the abundance that He has promised. Seek first the salvation that is available through a personal, passionate relationship with Christ, and then claim the joy, the peace, and the spiritual abundance that the Shepherd offers His sheep.

∞ *God loves you and wants you to experience peace and life—abundant and eternal.*

Billy Graham

∞ *Yes, we were created for His holy pleasure, but we will ultimately—if not immediately—find much pleasure in His pleasure.*

Beth Moore

WHEN ANGER IS OKAY

The face of the Lord is against those who do evil.

Psalm 34:16 NKJV

∞ Sometimes, anger can be a good thing. In the 21st chapter of Matthew, we are told how Christ responded when He confronted the evildoings of those who had invaded His Father's house of worship: "Then Jesus went into the temple of God and drove out all those who bought and sold in the temple, and overturned the tables of the money changers and the seats of those who sold doves. And He said to them, "It is written, 'My house shall be called a house of prayer,' but you have made it a 'den of thieves.'" (12-13 NKJV). Thus Jesus demonstrated that righteous indignation is an appropriate response to evil.

When you come face-to-face with the devil's handiwork, don't be satisfied to remain safely on the sidelines. Instead, follow in the footsteps of your Savior. Jesus never compromised with evil, and neither should you.

∞ *There is a holy anger, excited by zeal, that moves us to reprove with warmth those whom our mildness failed to correct.*

Jean Baptiste de la Salle

∞ *We cannot love God if we do not hate evil.*

St. Jerome

ACCOUNTABILITY TO GOD

We encouraged you, we urged you, and we insisted
that you live good lives for God, who calls you
to his glorious kingdom.

1 Thessalonians 2:12 NCV

∽ Here's something we should think about every day: some day, perhaps sooner than we imagine, we'll come face-to-face with our Heavenly Father, and we'll be called to account for our actions here on earth. Our personal histories will certainly not be surprising to God; He already knows everything about us. But the full scope of our activities may be surprising to us: some of us will be pleasantly surprised; others will not be.

Today, do whatever you can to ensure that your thoughts and your deeds are pleasing to your Creator. Because you will, at some point in the future, be called to account for your actions. And the future may be sooner than you think.

∽ *The cross that Jesus commands you and me to carry is the cross of submissive obedience to the will of God, even when His will includes suffering and hardship and things we don't want to do.*

Anne Graham Lotz

THE FUTILITY OF BLAME

The heart knows its own bitterness,
and a stranger does not share its joy.

Proverbs 14:10 NKJV

∞ Have you acquired the bad habit of blaming others for problems that you could or should solve yourself? If so, you are not only disobeying God's Word, you are also wasting your own precious time. To blame others for our own problems is the height of futility.

Blaming others is a favorite human pastime. Why? Because blaming is much easier than fixing, and criticizing others is so much easier than improving ourselves. So instead of solving our problems legitimately (by doing the work required to solve them) we are inclined to fret, to blame, and to criticize, while doing precious little else. When we do, our problems, quite predictably, remain unsolved.

So, instead of looking for someone to blame, look for something to fix, and then get busy fixing it. And as you consider your own situation, remember this: God has a way of helping those who help themselves, but He doesn't spend much time helping those who don't.

∞ *You'll never win the blame game, so why even bother to play?*

Marie T. Freeman

UNWELCOME CHANGES?

For unto us a Child is born, Unto us a Son is given;
And the government will be upon His shoulder. And His
name will be called Wonderful, Counselor, Mighty God,
Everlasting Father, Prince of Peace.

Isaiah 9:6 NKJV

∞ Life is often challenging, but as Christians, we should not be afraid. Are you facing difficult circumstances or unwelcome changes? If so, please remember that God is far bigger than any problem you may face. So, instead of worrying about life's inevitable challenges, put your faith in the Father and His only begotten Son: "Jesus Christ is the same yesterday, today, and forever" (Hebrews 13:8 NKJV). And remember: it is precisely because your Savior does not change that you can face your challenges with courage for today and hope for tomorrow.

God loves us, and He will protect us. In times of hardship, He will comfort us; in times of change, He will guide our steps. When we are troubled, or weak, or sorrowful, God is always with us. We must build our lives on the rock that cannot be moved...we must trust in God. Always.

∞ *One of the greatest ways God changes me is by bringing Scripture to mind that I have hidden deep in my heart. And, He always picks the right Scripture at the right time.*

Evelyn Christianson

Choosing Wisely

But the wisdom that is from above is first pure,
hen peaceable, gentle, willing to yield, full of mercy and
good fruits, without partiality and without hypocrisy.

James 3:17 NKJV

∞ Because we are creatures of free will, we make choices—lots of them. When we make choices that are pleasing to our Heavenly Father, we are blessed. When we make choices that cause us to walk in the footsteps of God's Son, we enjoy the abundance that Christ has promised to those who follow Him. But when make choices that are displeasing to God, we sow seeds that have the potential to bring forth a bitter harvest.

Today, as you encounter the challenges of everyday living, you will make hundreds of choices. Choose wisely. Make your thoughts and your actions pleasing to God. And remember: every choice that is displeasing to Him is the wrong choice—no exceptions.

∞ *We are either the masters or the victims of our attitudes. It is a matter of personal choice. Who we are today is the result of choices we made yesterday. Tomorrow, we will become what we choose today. To change means to choose to change.*

John Maxwell

THE PROMISE OF POWER

*When we were baptized, we were buried with Christ
and shared his death. So, just as Christ was raised from
the dead by the wonderful power of the Father,
we also can live a new life.*

Romans 6:4 NCV

∞ When you invite Christ to rule over your heart,
you avail yourself of His power. And make no mistake
about it: You and Christ, working together, can do
miraculous things. In fact, miraculous things are
exactly what Christ intends for you to do, but He
won't force you to do great things on His behalf. The
decision to become a full-fledged participant in His
power is a decision that you must make for yourself.

The words of John 14:12 make this promise: when
you put absolute faith in Christ, you can share in His
power. Today, trust the Savior's promise and expect a
miracle in His name.

∞ *The Christian life is not simply following principles
but being empowered to fulfill our purpose: knowing and
exalting Christ.*

Franklin Graham

∞ *The amount of power you experience to live
a victorious, triumphant Christian life is directly
proportional to the freedom you give the Spirit to be Lord
of your life!*

Anne Graham Lotz

THE PROMISE OF CONTENTMENT

I am not telling you this because I need anything.
I have learned to be satisfied with the things I have and
with everything that happens. I know how to live when
I am poor, and I know how to live when I have plenty.
I have learned the secret of being happy at
any time in everything that happens.

Philippians 4:11-12 NCV

∞ If we don't find contentment in God, we will never find it anywhere else. But, if we seek Him and obey Him, we will be blessed with an inner peace that is beyond human understanding. Genuine contentment is a gift from God to those who trust Him and follow His commandments.

Our modern world seems preoccupied with the search for happiness. We are bombarded with messages telling us that happiness depends upon the acquisition of material possessions. These messages are false. Enduring peace is not the result of our acquisitions; it is a spiritual gift from God to those who obey Him and accept His will.

When God dwells at the center of our lives, peace and contentment will belong to us just as surely as we belong to God.

∞ *True contentment comes from godliness in the heart, not from wealth in the hand.*

Warren Wiersbe

GOD CAN HANDLE IT

The Lord himself will go before you.
He will be with you; he will not leave you or forget you.
Don't be afraid and don't worry.

Deuteronomy 31:8 NCV

∞ The next time you find your courage tested to the limit, remember that God is as near as your next breath. He is your shield and your strength; He is your protector and your deliverer.

Life can be difficult and discouraging at times. During our darkest moments, God offers us strength and courage if we turn our hearts and our prayers to Him.

As believing Christians, we have every reason to live courageously. After all, the ultimate battle has already been fought and won on the cross at Calvary. But sometimes, because we are imperfect human beings who possess imperfect faith, we fall prey to fear and doubt. The answer to our fears, of course, is God.

Call upon Him in your hour of need and then be comforted. Whatever your challenge, whatever your trouble, God can handle it . . . and will!

∞ *If a person fears God, he or she has no reason to fear anything else. On the other hand, if a person does not fear God, then fear becomes a way of life.*

Beth Moore

TEACHING DISCIPLINE

Whoever accepts correction is on the way to life,
but whoever ignores correction will lead
others away from life.

Proverbs 10:17 NCV

∞ Wise parents teach their children the importance of discipline using both words and examples. Disciplined parents understand that God doesn't reward laziness or misbehavior. To the contrary, God expects His believers to lead lives that are above reproach. And, He punishes those who disobey His commandments.

In Proverbs 28:19, God's message is clear: "Those who work their land will have plenty of food, but the ones who chase empty dreams instead will end up poor." (NCV). When we work diligently and consistently, we can expect a bountiful harvest. But we must never expect the harvest to precede the labor. First, we must lead lives of discipline and obedience; then, we will reap the never-ending rewards that God has promised . . . and that's precisely we must teach our children.

∞ *If one examines the secret behind a championship football team, a magnificent orchestra, or a successful business, the principal ingredient is invariably discipline.*

James Dobson

CELEBRATING OTHERS

So encourage each other and give each other strength,
just as you are doing now.

1 Thessalonians 5:11 NCV

∞ Do you delight in the victories of others? You should. Each day provides countless opportunities to encourage others and to praise their good works. When you do so, you not only spread seeds of joy and happiness, you also obey the commandments of God's Holy Word.

As Christians, we are called upon to spread the Good News of Christ, and we are also called to spread a message of encouragement and hope to the world.

Today, let us be cheerful Christians with smiles on our faces and encouraging words on our lips. By blessing others, we also bless ourselves, and, at the same time, we do honor to the One who gave His life for us.

∞ *My special friends, who know me so well and love me anyway, give me daily encouragement to keep on.*

Emilie Barnes

∞ *A lot of people have gone further than they thought they could because someone else thought they could.*

Zig Ziglar

Your Eternal Journey

*Most assuredly, I say to you, he who hears My word
and believes in Him who sent Me has everlasting life,
and shall not come into judgment,
but has passed from death into life.*

John 5:24 NKJV

∞ Eternal life is not an event that begins when you die. Eternal life begins when you invite Jesus into your heart right here on earth. So it's important to remember that God's plans for you are not limited to the ups and downs of everyday life. If you've allowed Jesus to reign over your heart, you've already begun your eternal journey.

As mere mortals, our vision for the future, like our lives here on earth, is limited. God's vision is not burdened by such limitations: His plans extend throughout all eternity.

Let us praise the Creator for His priceless gift, and let us share the Good News with all who cross our paths. We return our Father's love by accepting His grace and by sharing His message and His love. When we do, we are blessed here on earth and throughout all eternity.

∞ *Your choice to either receive or reject the Lord Jesus Christ will determine where you spend eternity.*

Anne Graham Lotz

GOD AND FAMILY

Let the word of Christ dwell in you richly in all wisdom,
teaching and admonishing one another in psalms
and hymns and spiritual songs, singing with grace
in your hearts to the Lord.

Colossians 3:16 NKJV

∞ We live in a world where temptation and danger seem to lurk on every street corner. Parents and children alike have good reason to be watchful. These are difficult days for our nation and for our families. But, thankfully, God is bigger than all of our challenges. God loves us and protects us. In times of trouble, he comforts us; in times of sorrow, He dries our tears. When we are troubled, or weak, or sorrowful, God is as near as our next breath.

Are you concerned for the wellbeing of your family? You are not alone. But, despite the evils of our time, God remains steadfast. Even in these difficult days, no problem is too big for God.

∞ *It matters that we should be true to one another, be loyal to what is a family—only a little family in the great Household, but still a family, with family love alive in it and action as a living bond.*

Amy Carmichael

PEACE TO YOU

Peace, peace to you, and peace to your helpers!
For your God helps you.

1 Chronicles 12:18 NKJV

∞ Sometimes, our struggles are simply manifestations of the inner conflict that we feel when we stray from God's path.

Have you found the genuine peace that can be yours through Christ? Or are you still rushing after the illusion of "peace and happiness" that the world promises but cannot deliver? Today, as a gift to yourself and to your loved ones, claim the inner peace that is your spiritual birthright: the peace of Jesus Christ. It is offered freely; it has been paid for in full; it is yours for the asking. So ask. And then share.

Earthly peace can, and should, be yours. But the spiritual peace that stems from your personal relationship with Jesus must be yours if you are to receive the eternal abundance of our Lord. Claim that abundance today.

∞ *If the Living Logos of God has the power to create and sustain the universe, He is more than able to sustain your marriage and your ministry, your faith and your finances, your hope and your health.*

Anne Graham Lotz

THE CHOICE TO FORGIVE

*"You have heard that it was said, 'You shall love your
neighbor and hate your enemy.' But I say to you, love
your enemies, bless those who curse you, do good to
those who hate you, and pray for those who spitefully use
you and persecute you, that you may be
sons of your Father in heaven."*

Matthew 5:43-45 NKJV

∞ Life is filled with choices, and one of the most
important choices we can ever make is the choice to
forgive. And make no mistake: forgiveness is a choice.
We can either choose to forgive those who have
injured us, or not. When we obey God by offering
forgiveness to His children, we are blessed. But when
we allow bitterness and resentment to poison our
hearts, we are tortured by our own shortsightedness.

Do you harbor resentment against anyone? If so,
you are faced with an important decision: whether
or not to forgive the person who has hurt you. God's
instructions are clear: He commands you to forgive.
And the time to forgive is now because tomorrow
may be too late . . . for you.

∞ *Jesus is the only One Who makes not only our sins but
also the sins of others against us forgivable.*

Anne Graham Lotz

FREELY GIVE

So let each one give as he purposes in his heart, not grudgingly or of necessity; for God loves a cheerful giver.

2 Corinthians 9:7 NKJV

∞ The words are familiar to those who study God's Word: "Freely you have received, freely give." As followers of Christ, we have been given so much by God. In return, we must give freely of our time, our possessions, our testimonies, and our love.

Your salvation was earned at a terrible price: Christ gave His life for you on the cross at Calvary. Christ's gift is priceless, yet when you accept Jesus as your personal Savior, His gift of eternal life costs you nothing. From those to whom much has been given, much is required. And because you have received the gift of salvation, you are now called by God to be a cheerful, generous steward of the gifts He has placed under your care.

Today and every day, let Christ's words be your guide and let His eternal love fill your heart. When you do, your stewardship will be a reflection of your love for Him, and that's exactly as it should be. After all, He loved you first.

∞ *As faithful stewards of what we have, ought we not to give earnest thought to our staggering surplus?*

Elisabeth Elliot

THE GIFT OF SALVATION

*For by grace you have been saved through faith,
and that not of yourselves; it is the gift of God,
not of works, lest anyone should boast.*

Ephesians 2:8-9 NKJV

∞ God's grace is the ultimate gift, and we owe to Him the ultimate in thanksgiving. God has given us so many gifts, but none can compare with the gift of salvation. We have not earned our salvation; it is a gift from God. When we accept Christ into our hearts, we are saved by His grace.

Let us praise the Creator for His priceless gift, and let us share the Good News with all who cross our paths. We return our Father's love by accepting His grace and by sharing His message and His love. When we do, we are eternally blessed . . . and the Father smiles.

∞ *The grace of God is sufficient for all our needs, for every problem, and for every difficulty, for every broken heart, and for every human sorrow.*

Peter Marshall

∞ God "longs to be gracious" to us (Isaiah 30:18), and He carries out His judgment against our sin with holy sorrow, intending His discipline to be a vehicle of mercy toward us.

Nancy Groom

SENSING HIS PRESENCE

Where can I go from Your Spirit? Or where can
I flee from Your presence? If I ascend into heaven,
You are there; If I make my bed in hell, behold, You are
there. If I take the wings of the morning, And dwell in
the uttermost parts of the sea, Even there Your hand
shall lead me, And Your right hand shall hold me.

Psalms 139:7-10 NKJV

∽ If God doesn't feel close, guess who moved? The answer to that question, of course, has nothing to do with God and everything to do with us.

When we begin each day on our knees, in praise and worship to Him, God often seems very near indeed. But, if we ignore God's presence or—worse yet—rebel against it altogether, the world in which we live becomes a spiritual wasteland.

Today, and every day hereafter, thank God and praise Him. He is the Giver of all things good. Wherever you are, whether you are happy or sad, victorious or vanquished, celebrate God's presence. And be comforted. For He is here.

∽ *The tender eyes of God perpetually see us. He has never stopped noticing.*

Angela Thomas

∽ *God is nearer to me than I am to myself; my existence depends on the nearness and the presence of God.*

Meister Eckhart

ENTRUSTING OUR LIVES TO HIM

"Father, if it is Your will, take this cup away from Me;
nevertheless not My will, but Yours, be done."

Luke 22:42 NKJV

෨ As human beings with limited understanding, we can never fully comprehend the will of God. But as believers in a benevolent God, we must always trust the will of our Heavenly Father.

Before His crucifixion, Jesus went to the Mount of Olives and opened His heart to the Father. Jesus knew of the torture that He must soon endure, but He also knew that God's will must be done.

We, like our Savior, face trials that bring fear and trembling to the very depths of our souls, but like Christ, we, too, must ultimately seek God's will, not our own. When we entrust our lives to Him completely and without reservation, He gives us the strength to meet any challenge, the courage to face any trial, and the wisdom to live in His righteousness.

෨ *The will of God is the most delicious and delightful thing in the universe.*

Hannah Whitall Smith

෨ *To know the will of God is the greatest knowledge! To do the will of God is the greatest achievement.*

George W. Truett

ABANDONING BAD HABITS

Do not be deceived:
"Evil company corrupts good habits."

1 Corinthians 15:33 NKJV

∞ If you sincerely desire to improve your spiritual health, you must honestly examine the habits that make up the fabric of your day. It's an old saying and a true one: First, you make your habits, and then your habits make you. Some habits will inevitably bring you closer to God; other habits will lead you away from the path He has chosen for you. You must abandon those habits that are displeasing to God.

If you trust God, and if you keep asking for His help, He can transform your life. If you sincerely ask Him to help you, the same God who created the universe will help you defeat the harmful habits that have heretofore defeated you. So, if at first you don't succeed, keep praying. God is listening, and He's ready to help you become a better person if you ask Him . . . so ask today.

∞ *Begin to be now what you will be hereafter.*

St. Jerome

∞ *If you want to form a new habit, get to work. If you want to break a bad habit, get on your knees.*

Marie T. Freeman

HOPE FOR TODAY

*You have this faith and love because of your hope,
and what you hope for is kept safe for you in heaven.
You learned about this hope when you heard the message
about the truth, the Good News.*

Colossians 1:5 NCV

∞ Despite God's promises, despite Christ's love, and despite our countless blessings, we frail human beings can still lose hope from time to time. When we do, we need the encouragement of Christian friends, the life-changing power of prayer, and the healing truth of God's Holy Word. If we find ourselves falling into the spiritual traps of worry and discouragement, we should seek the healing touch of Jesus and the encouraging words of fellow Christians. Even though this world can be a place of trials and struggles, God has promised us peace, joy, and eternal life if we give ourselves to Him. And, of course, God keeps His promises today, tomorrow, and forever.

∞ *The most profane word we use is "hopeless." When you say a situation or person is hopeless, you are slamming the door in the face of God.*

Kathy Troccoli

∞ *What oxygen is to the lungs, such is hope to the meaning of life.*

Emil Brunner

A Dose of Laughter

A happy heart is like good medicine.

Proverbs 17:22 NCV

∞ Laughter is medicine for the soul, but sometimes, amid the stresses of the day, we forget to take our medicine. Instead of viewing our world with a mixture of optimism and humor, we allow worries and distractions to rob us of the joy that God intends for our lives. Today, as you go about your daily activities, approach life with a smile and a chuckle. After all, God created laughter for a reason...and Father indeed knows best. So do yourself a favor and laugh!

∞ *Laughter dulls the sharpest pain and flattens out the greatest stress. To share it is to give a gift of health.*

Barbara Johnson

∞ *Laughter can relieve tension, soothe the pain of disappointment, and strengthen the spirit for the formidable tasks that always lie ahead.*

Dwight D. Eisenhower

∞ *Mirth is God's medicine. Everybody ought to bathe in it.*

Henry Ward Beecher

BEYOND MATERIALISM

For what will it profit a man if he gains the whole world,
and loses his own soul? Or what will a man
give in exchange for his soul?

Mark 8:36-37 NKJV

⟄ In our modern society, we need money to live. But as Christians, we must never make the acquisition of money the central focus of our lives. Money is a tool, but it should never overwhelm our sensibilities. The focus of life must be squarely on things spiritual, not things material.

Whenever we place our love for material possessions above our love for God—or when we yield to the countless other temptations of everyday living—we find ourselves engaged in a struggle between good and evil. Let us respond to this struggle by freeing ourselves from that subtle yet powerful temptation: the temptation to love the world more than we love God.

⟄ *We own too many things that aren't worth owning.*

Marie T. Freeman

⟄ *The socially prescribed affluent, middle-class lifestyle has become so normative in our churches that we discern little conflict between it and the Christian lifestyle prescribed in the New Testament.*

Tony Compolo

On Being an Optimistic Christian

Make me hear joy and gladness.

Psalm 51:8 NKJV

◎ To be a pessimistic Christian is a contradiction in terms, yet sometimes even the most devout Christians fall prey to fear, doubt, and discouragement. But, God has a different plan for our lives. The comforting words of the 23rd Psalm remind us of God's blessings. In response to His grace, we should strive to focus our thoughts on things that are pleasing to Him, not upon things that are evil, discouraging, or frustrating.

So, the next time you find yourself mired in the pit of pessimism, remember God's Word and redirect your thoughts. This world is God's creation; look for the best in it, and trust Him to take care of the rest.

◎ *Great hopes make great men.*

Thomas Fuller

◎ *The game was to just find something about everything to be glad about—no matter what it was. You see, when you're hunting for the glad things, you sort of forget the other kind.*

Eleanor H. Porter

◎ *Be hopeful! For tomorrow has never happened before.*

Robert Schuller

THE POWER OF PERSEVERANCE

There is one thing I always do. Forgetting the past and
straining toward what is ahead, I keep trying to reach
the goal and get the prize for which God called me . . . .

Philippians 3:13–14 NCV

∞ A well-lived life calls for preparation,
determination, and, of course, lots of perseverance.
As an example of perfect perseverance, we Christians
need look no further than our Savior, Jesus Christ.
Jesus finished what He began. Despite His suffering,
despite the shame of the cross, Jesus was steadfast in
His faithfulness to God. We, too, must remain faithful,
especially during times of hardship. Sometimes, God
may answer our prayers with silence, and when He
does, we must patiently persevere.

Are you facing a tough situation? If so, remember
this: whatever your problem, God can handle it. Your
job is to keep persevering until He does.

∞ *If things are tough, remember that every flower that*
ever bloomed had to go through a whole lot of dirt to get
there.

Barbara Johnson

∞ *Only the man who follows the command of Jesus*
single-mindedly and unresistingly lets his yoke rest upon
him, finds his burden easy, and under its gentle pressure
receives the power to persevere in the right way.

Dietrich Bonhoeffer

First Things First

*The thing you should want most is God's kingdom
and doing what God wants. Then all these other things
you need will be given to you.*

Matthew 6:33 NCV

℥ Have you asked God to help prioritize Your day or are you muddling along without His help? Have you asked Him for guidance and for the courage to do the things that need to be done, or are you seeking guidance only from the person in the mirror? If you're genuinely consulting God, then you're continually inviting your Creator to reveal Himself in a variety of ways. And if you wish to be a thoughtful, productive follower of Christ, you must do no less.

When you allow God to reign over your heart, He will honor you with spiritual blessings that are simply too numerous to count. So, as you plan for the day ahead, make God's will your ultimate priority. When you do, your daily to-do list will take care of itself.

℥ *The moment you wake up each morning, all your wishes and hopes for the day rush at you like wild animals. And the first job each morning consists in shoving it all back; in listening to that other voice, taking that other point of view, letting that other, larger, stronger, quieter life coming flowing in.*

C. S. Lewis

ACCUMULATING WISDOM

But also for this very reason, giving all diligence,
add to your faith virtue, to virtue knowledge.

2 Peter 1:5 NKJV

∞ Wisdom is like a savings account: If you add to it consistently, then eventually you will have accumulated a great sum. The secret to success is consistency.

Do you seek wisdom for yourself and for your family? Then keep learning and keep motivating them to do likewise. The ultimate source of wisdom, of course, is the Word of God. When you study God's Word and live according to His commandments, you will become wise.

∞ *Don't expect wisdom to come into your life like great chunks of rock on a conveyor belt. Wisdom comes privately from God as a byproduct of right decisions, godly reactions, and the application of spiritual principles to daily circumstances.*

Charles Swindoll

∞ *If we neglect the Bible, we cannot expect to benefit from the wisdom and direction that result from knowing God's Word.*

Vonette Bright

PURE THOUGHTS

Those who are pure in their thinking are happy,
because they will be with God.

Matthew 5:8 NCV

⟳ How easy it is to focus on our worries and fears, a focus that can leave us depressed and demoralized.

Paul Valéry observed, "We hope vaguely but dread precisely." He was right. All too often, we allow the worries of everyday life to overwhelm our thoughts and cloud our vision. What's needed is clearer perspective, renewed faith, and a different focus.

When we focus on the frustrations of today or the uncertainties of tomorrow, we rob ourselves of peace in the present moment. But, when we focus on God's grace, and when we trust in the ultimate wisdom of God's plan for our lives, our worries no longer tyrannize us.

Today, remember that God is infinitely greater than the challenges that you face. Remember also that your thoughts are profoundly powerful, so guard them accordingly.

⟳ *No more imperfect thoughts. No more sad memories. No more ignorance. My redeemed body will have a redeemed mind. Grant me a foretaste of that perfect mind as you mirror your thoughts in me today.*

Joni Eareckson Tada

JUST PASSING THROUGH

For whatever is born of God overcomes the world.
And this is the victory that has
overcome the world—our faith.

1 John 5:4 NKJV

Sometimes the troubles of this old world are easier to tolerate when we remind ourselves that heaven is our true home. An old hymn contains the words, "This world is not my home; I'm just passing through." Thank goodness!

This crazy world can be a place of trouble and danger. Thankfully, God has offered you a permanent home in heaven, a place of unimaginable glory, a place that your Heavenly Father has already prepared for you,

In John 16:33, Jesus tells us He has overcome the troubles of this world. We should trust Him, and we should obey His commandments. When we do, we can withstand any problem, knowing that our troubles are temporary, but that heaven is not.

All those who look to draw their satisfaction from the wells of the world—pleasure, popularity, position, possessions, politics, power, prestige, finances, family, friends, fame, fortune, career, children, church, clubs, sports, sex, success, recognition, reputation, religion, education, entertainment, exercise, honors, health, hobbies—will soon be thirsty again!

Anne Graham Lotz

Overcoming Stress

Then they cried out to the Lord in their trouble,
and He saved them out of their distresses.

Psalm 107:13 NKJV

∞ Elisabeth Elliot writes, "If my life is surrendered to God, all is well. Let me not grab it back, as though it were in peril in His hand but would be safer in mine!" These words apply to all of us.

We all know that stressful days are an inevitable fact of modern life. And how do we deal with the challenges of being busy in a demanding, 21st-century world? By turning our days and our lives over to God. May we give our lives, our hopes, and our prayers to the Father, and, by doing so, accept His will and His peace.

∞ *Satan does some of his worst work on exhausted Christians when nerves are frayed and the mind is faint.*

Vance Havner

∞ *When frustrations develop into problems that stress you out, the best way to cope is to stop, catch your breath, and do something for yourself, not out of selfishness, but out of wisdom.*

Barbara Johnson

TRUSTING GOD'S LEADING

My brethren, count it all joy when you fall into various
trials, knowing that the testing of your faith produces
patience. But let patience have its perfect work,
that you may be perfect and complete, lacking nothing.

James 1:2-4 NKJV

∞ Whether we realize it or not, times of adversity can be times of intense personal and spiritual growth. Our difficult days are also times when we can learn and relearn some of life's most important lessons.

The next time you experience a difficult moment, a difficult day, or a difficult year, ask yourself this question: Where is God leading me? In times of struggle and sorrow, you can be certain that God is leading you to a place of His choosing. Your duty is to watch, to pray, to listen, and to follow.

∞ *When I feel like circumstances are spiraling downward in my life, God taught me that whether I'm right side up or upside down, I need to turn those circumstances over to Him. He is the only one who can bring balance into my life.*

Carole Lewis

∞ *Many men owe the grandeur of their lives to their tremendous difficulties.*

C. H. Spurgeon

TERMINATING THE TANTRUMS

*Don't make friends with quick-tempered people or spend
time with those who have bad tempers. If you do,
you will be like them. Then you will be in real danger.*

Proverbs 22:24-25 NCV

☞ If you've allowed anger to become a regular visitor at your house, today you must pray for wisdom, for patience, and for a heart that is so filled with love and forgiveness that it contains no room for bitterness. Temper tantrums are usually unproductive, unattractive, unforgettable, and unnecessary. Perhaps that's why Proverbs 16:32 states that, "Controlling your temper is better than capturing a city" (NCV).

God will help you terminate your tantrums if you ask Him to. And God can help you perfect your ability to be patient if you ask Him to. So ask Him, and then wait patiently for the ever-more-patient you to arrive.

☞ *Never do anything when you are in a fit of temper, for you will do everything wrong.*

Baltasar Gracián

☞ *Anger is a kind of temporary madness.*

St. Basil the Great

☞ *The fire of anger, if not quenched by loving forgiveness, will spread and defile and destroy the work of God.*

Warren Wiersbe

THE RIGHT KIND OF BEHAVIOR

Now by this we know that we know Him,
if we keep His commandments.

1 John 2:3 NKJV

❧ When we live righteously and according to God's commandments, He blesses us in ways that we cannot fully understand. When we seek righteousness in our own lives—and when we seek the companionship of those who do likewise—we reap the spiritual rewards that God intends for us to enjoy. When we behave ourselves in a godly way, we honor our Creator.

Today, as you fulfill your responsibilities, hold fast that which is good, and associate yourself with believers who behave themselves in like fashion. When you do, your good works will serve as a powerful example for others and as a worthy offering to your Father in Heaven.

❧ *Christianity says we were created by a righteous God to flourish and be exhilarated in a righteous environment. God has "wired" us in such a way that the more righteous we are, the more we'll actually enjoy life.*

Bill Hybels

❧ *In the fulfillment of your duties, let your intentions be so pure that you reject from your actions any other motive than the glory of God and the salvation of souls.*

Angela Merici

PRIORITIES . . . MOMENT BY MOMENT

*Love never hurts a neighbor, so loving is obeying all the
law. Do this because we live in an important time.
It is now time for you to wake up from your sleep . . . .*

Romans 13:10-11 NCV

❋ Each waking moment holds the potential to think a
creative thought or offer a heartfelt prayer. So even if
you're a person with too many demands and too few
hours in which to meet them, don't panic. Instead, be
comforted in the knowledge that when you sincerely
seek to discover God's priorities for your life, He will
provide answers in marvelous and surprising ways.

Remember: this is the day that God has made and
that He has filled it with countless opportunities to
love, to serve, and to seek His guidance. Seize those
opportunities. And as a gift to yourself, to your family,
and to the world, slow down and establish clear
priorities that are pleasing to God. When you do,
you will earn the inner peace that is your spiritual
birthright: the peace of Jesus Christ. It is yours for the
asking. So ask . . . and be thankful.

❋ *In our tense, uptight society where folks are rushing
to make appointments they have already missed, a good
laugh can be a refreshing as a cup of cold water in the
desert.*

Barbara Johnson

HOPE DURING TIMES OF CHANGE

Therefore do not worry about tomorrow,
for tomorrow will worry about its own things.
Sufficient for the day is its own trouble.

Matthew 6:34 NKJV

❊ There is no doubt. Your world is constantly changing. So today's question is this: How will you manage all those changes?" Will you do your best and trust God with the rest, or will you spend fruitless hours worrying about things you can't control, while doing precious little else? The answer to these simple questions will help determine the direction and quality of your life.

The best way to confront change is head-on . . . and with God by your side. The same God who created the universe will protect you if you ask Him, so ask Him—and then serve Him with willing hands and a trusting heart. When you do, you may rest assured that while the world changes moment by moment, God's love endures—unfathomable and unchanging—forever.

❊ *When we are young, change is a treat, but as we grow older, change becomes a threat. But when Jesus Christ is in control of your life, you need never fear change or decay.*

Warren Wiersbe

Choosing to Please God

I am offering you life or death, blessings or curses.
Now, choose life! . . . To choose life is to love the Lord
your God, obey him, and stay close to him.

Deuteronomy 30:19-20 NCV

❧ Whom will you try to please today: God or man?
Your primary obligation is not to please imperfect
men and women. Your obligation is to strive
diligently to meet the expectations of an all-knowing
and perfect God.

Sometimes, because you're an imperfect human
being, you may become so wrapped up in meeting
society's expectations that you fail to focus on
God's expectations. To do so is a mistake of major
proportions—don't make it. Instead, seek God's
guidance as you focus your energies on becoming
the best "you" that you can possibly be. And, when
it comes to matters of conscience, seek approval not
from your peers, but from your Creator.

Trust God always. Love Him always. Praise Him
always. And make choices that please Him. Always.

❧ *I do not know how the Spirit of Christ performs it, but*
He brings us choices through which we constantly change,
fresh and new, into His likeness.

Joni Eareckson Tada

A PLACE OF WORSHIP

If two or three people come together in my name,
I am there with them.

Matthew 18:20 NCV

❋ Where do we worship? In our hearts or in our church? The answer is both. As Christians who have been saved by a loving, compassionate Creator, we are compelled not only to worship the Creator in our hearts but also to worship Him in the presence of fellow believers.

We live in a world that is teeming with temptations and distractions—a world where good and evil struggle in a constant battle to win our hearts and souls. Our challenge, of course, is to ensure that we cast our lot on the side of God. One way to ensure that we do so is by the practice of regular, purposeful worship with our families. When we worship God faithfully and fervently, we are blessed.

❋ *The house of God is not a safe place. It is a cross where time and eternity meet, and where we are—or should be—challenged to live more vulnerably, more interdependently.*

Madeleine L'Engle

❋ *The New Testament does not envisage solitary religion; some kind of regular assembly for worship and instruction is everywhere taken for granted in the epistles.*

C. S. Lewis

NEW AND APPROVED

If anyone belongs to Christ, there is a new creation.
The old things have gone; everything is made new!

2 Corinthians 5:17 NCV

❋ The Bible clearly teaches that when we welcome Christ into our hearts, we become new creations through Him. Our challenge, of course, is to behave ourselves like new creations.

Think, for a moment, about the "old" you, the person you were before you invited Christ to reign over your heart. Now, think about the "new" you, the person you have become since then. Is there a difference between the "old" you and the "new and improved" version? There should be! And that difference should be noticeable not only to you but also to others.

When we expereince true conversion, God fills our hearts, He blesses our endeavors, and transforms our lives . . . forever.

❋ *No man is ever the same after God has laid His hand upon him.*

A. W. Tozer

❋ *The whole idea of belonging to Christ is to look less and less like we used to and more and more like Him.*

Angela Thomas

CRITICS BEWARE

Judge not, and you shall not be judged.
Condemn not, and you shall not be condemned.
Forgive, and you will be forgiven.

Luke 6:37 NKJV

❋ From experience, we know that it is easier to criticize than to correct. And we know that it is easier to find faults than solutions. Yet the urge to criticize others remains a powerful temptation for most of us. Our task, as obedient believers, is to break the twin habits of negative thinking and critical speech.

Negativity is highly contagious: we give it to others who, in turn, give it back to us. This cycle can be broken by positive thoughts, heartfelt prayers, and encouraging words. As thoughtful servants of a loving God, we can use the transforming power of Christ's love to break the chains of negativity. And we should.

❋ *It takes less sense to criticize than to do anything else.*

Sam Jones

❋ *Do not think of the faults of others but of what is good in them and faulty in yourself.*

St. Teresa of Avila

❋ *Any fool can criticize, condemn, and complain—and most fools do.*

Dale Carnegie

DISCIPLINE YOURSELF

*But do not follow foolish stories that disagree with
God's truth, but train yourself to serve God.*

1 Timothy 4:7 NCV

❋ Are you a self-disciplined person? If so, congratulations . . . your disciplined approach to life can help
you can build a more meaningful relationship with
God. Why? Because God expects all His believers
(including you) to lead lives of disciplined obedience
to Him . . . and He rewards those believers who do.

Sometimes, it's hard to be dignified and
disciplined. Why? Because you live in a world where
many prominent people want you to believe that
dignified, self-disciplined behavior is going out of
style. But don't deceive yourself: self-discipline never
goes out of style.

Your greatest accomplishments will probably
require plenty of work and a heaping helping of self-
discipline—which, by the way, is perfectly fine with
God. After all, He knows that you're up to the task,
and He has big plans for you. God will do His part
to fulfill those plans, and the rest, of course, depends
upon you.

❋ *Real freedom means to welcome the responsibility
it brings, to welcome the God-control it requires, to
welcome the discipline that results, to welcome the
maturity it creates.*

Eugenia Price

SHARING WORDS OF HOPE

*Let us think about each other and help each other
to show love and do good deeds.*

Hebrews 10:24 NCV

❦ Hope, like other human emotions, is contagious. When we associate with hope-filled Christians, we are encouraged by their faith and optimism. But, if we spend too much time in the company of naysayers and pessimists, our attitudes, like theirs, tend to be cynical and negative.

Are you a hopeful, optimistic, encouraging believer? And do you associate with like-minded people? Hopefully so. As a faithful follower of the One from Galilee, you have every reason to be hopeful, and you have every reason to share your hopes with others. So today, look for reasons to celebrate God's endless blessings. And while you're at it, look for people who will join you in the celebration. You'll be better for their company, and they'll be better for yours.

❦ *The glory of friendship is not the outstretched hand, or the kindly smile, or the joy of companionship. It is the spiritual inspiration that comes to one when he discovers that someone else believes in him and is willing to trust him with his friendship.*

Corrie ten Boom

WE ARE ALL ROLE MODELS

You are the light that gives light to the world.
In the same way, you should be a light for other people.
Live so that they will see the good things you do
and will praise your Father in heaven.

Matthew 5:14,16 NCV

❧ All of us are examples—examples that should be emulated . . . or not. Hopefully, the lives we lead and the choices we make will serve as enduring examples of the spiritual abundance that is available to all who worship God and obey His commandments.

Ask yourself this question: Are you the kind of role model that you would want to emulate? If so, congratulations. But if certain aspects of your behavior could stand improvement, the best day to begin your self-improvement regimen is this one. Because whether you realize it or not, people you love are watching your behavior, and they're learning how to live. You owe it to them—and to yourself—to live righteously and well.

❧ *Be sure that you first preach by the way you live. If you do not, people will notice that you say one thing, but live otherwise, and your words will bring only cynical laughter and a derisive shake of the head.*

Charles Cardinal Borromeo

GOD'S GIFT OF FAMILY

You must choose for yourselves today whom you
will serve . . . as for me and my family,
we will serve the Lord.

Joshua 24:15 NCV

❋ No family is perfect, and neither is yours. But, despite the inevitable challenges and hurt feelings of family life, your clan is God's gift to you.

In the life of every family, there are moments of frustration and disappointment. Lots of them. But, for those who are lucky enough to live in the presence of a close-knit, caring clan, the rewards far outweigh the frustrations.

That little band of men, women, kids, and babies is a priceless treasure on temporary loan from the Father above. Give thanks to the Giver for the gift of family…and act accordingly.

❋ *The only true source of meaning in life is found in love for God and his son Jesus Christ, and love for mankind, beginning with our own families.*

James Dobson

❋ *Money can build or buy a house. Add love to that, and you have a home. Add God to that, and you have a temple. You have "a little colony of the kingdom of heaven."*

Anne Ortland

FIT TO SERVE

*Therefore, whether you eat or drink, or whatever
you do, do all to the glory of God.*

1 Corinthians 10:31 NKJV

❋ God has a plan for every aspect of your life, and His
plan includes provisions for your physical health. But,
He expects you to do your fair share of the work!

We live in a world in which leisure is glorified and
consumption is commercialized. But God has other
plans. He did not create us for lives of gluttony or
laziness; He created us for far greater things.

In a world that is chock-full of tasty temptations,
you may find it all too easy to make unhealthy
choices. Your challenge, of course, is to resist those
unhealthy temptations by every means you can,
including prayer. And rest assured: when you ask for
God's help, He will give it.

❋ *We have a world to explore and master, and we can't
do it if our bodies are accumulating fat and our muscles,
joints, and internal organs are breaking down. We need
exercise.*

Dr. Jordan S. Rubin

❋ *Our primary motivation should not be for more energy
or to avoid a heart attack but to please God with our
bodies.*

Carole Lewis

GOD'S FORGIVENESS

If we confess our sins, He is faithful and just to forgive us our sins and to cleanse us from all unrighteousness.

1 John 1:9 NKJV

❖ The Bible promises you this: When you ask God for forgiveness, He will give it. No questions asked; no explanations required.

God's power to forgive, like His love, is infinite. Despite your sins, God offers immediate forgiveness. And it's time to take Him up on His offer.

When it comes to forgiveness, God doesn't play favorites and neither should you. You should forgive all the people who have harmed you (not just the people who have asked for forgiveness or the ones who have made restitution). Complete forgiveness is God's way, and it should be your way, too. Anything less is not enough.

❖ *The sequence of forgiveness and then repentance, rather than repentance and then forgiveness, is crucial for understanding the gospel of grace.*

Brennan Manning

❖ *For God is, indeed, a wonderful Father who longs to pour out His mercy upon us, and whose majesty is so great that He can transform us from deep within.*

Teresa of Avila

HIS GENEROSITY . . . AND YOURS

But God demonstrates His own love toward us, in that
while we were still sinners, Christ died for us.

Romans 5:8 NKJV

❦ Christ showed His generous love for us by willingly
sacrificing His own life so that we might have eternal
life. We, as Christ's followers, are challenged to share
His love. And, when we walk each day with Jesus—
and obey the commandments found in God's Holy
Word—we are worthy ambassadors for Him.

Just as Christ has been—and will always be—the
ultimate friend to His flock, so should we be Christlike
in our love and generosity to those in need. When we
share the love of Christ, we share a priceless gift. As
His servants, we must do no less.

❦ *The measure of a life, after all, is not its duration but*
its donation.

Corrie ten Boom

❦ *The world says, the more you take, the more you have.*
Christ says, the more you give, the more you are.

Frederick Buechner

❦ *The happiest and most joyful people are those who give*
money and serve.

Dave Ramsey

BLESSED FOREVER

For all have sinned, and fall short of the glory of God,
being justified freely by His grace through
the redemption that is in Christ Jesus....

Romans 3:23-24 NKJV

❋ Someone has said that GRACE stands for God's Redemption At Christ's Expense. It's true—God sent His Son so that we might be redeemed from our sins. In doing so, our Heavenly Father demonstrated His infinite mercy and His infinite love. We have received countless gifts from God, but none can compare with the gift of salvation. God's grace is the ultimate gift, and we owe Him the ultimate in thanksgiving.

The gift of eternal life is the priceless possession of everyone who accepts God's Son as Lord and Savior. We return our Savior's love by welcoming Him into our hearts and sharing His message and His love. When we do so, we are blessed not today and forever.

❋ *There is no secret that can separate you from God's love; there is no secret that can separate you from His blessings; there is no secret that is worth keeping from His grace.*

Serita Ann Jakes

❋ *God doesn't call the qualified, He qualifies the called.*

Anonymous

WITH YOU ALWAYS

You will teach me how to live a holy life.
Being with you will fill me with joy; at your right hand
I will find pleasure forever.

Psalm 16:11 NCV

❦ Do you ever wonder if God is really here? If so, you're not the first person to think such thoughts. In fact, some of the biggest heroes in the Bible had their doubts—and so, perhaps, will you. But when questions arise and doubts begin to creep into your mind, remember this: You can talk with God any time. In fact, He's right here, right now, listening to your thoughts and prayers, watching over your every move.

Sometimes, you will allow yourself to become very busy, and that's when you may be tempted to ignore God. But, when you quiet yourself long enough to acknowledge His presence, God will touch your heart and restore your spirits. By the way, He's ready to talk right now. Are you?

❦ *When we are in the presence of God, removed from distractions, we are able to hear him more clearly, and a secure environment has been established for the young and broken places in our hearts to surface.*

John Eldredge

SEEKING HIS WILL

Teach me to do Your will, for You are my God;
Your Spirit is good. Lead me in the land of uprightness.

Psalm 143:10 NKJV

❖ God has a plan for our world and for our lives—He does not do things by accident. God is willful and intentional, but we cannot always understand His purposes. Why? Because we are mortal beings with limited understanding. And although we cannot fully comprehend the will of God, we should always trust the will of God.

As this day unfolds, seek God's will and obey His Word. When you entrust your life to Him without reservation, He will give you the courage meet any challenge, the strength to endure any trial, and the wisdom to live in His righteousness and in His peace.

❖ *"If the Lord will" is not just a statement on a believer's lips; it is the constant attitude of his heart.*

Warren Wiersbe

❖ *Faith will not always get for us what we want, but it will get what God wants us to have.*

Vance Havner

SEEKING GOD AND FINDING HAPPINESS

Happy is he who has the God of Jacob for his help,
whose hope is in the Lord his God.

Psalm 146:5 NKJV

❧ Circumstances don't make us happy. Our attitude and our thoughts determine how happy we'll be. And make no mistake: happiness is indeed a choice.

When we choose to turn our thoughts to God, to His gifts, and to His glorious creation, we experience the joy that God intends for His children. But, when we focus on the negative aspects of life, we suffer needlessly.

Do you sincerely want to be a happy Christian? Then set your mind and your heart upon God's love and His grace. The fullness of life in Christ is available to all who seek it and claim it. Count yourself among that number. Seek first the salvation that is available through a personal relationship with Jesus Christ, and then claim the joy, the peace, and the spiritual abundance that the Good Shepherd offers to His flock.

❧ *God has charged Himself with full responsibility for our eternal happiness and stands ready to take over the management of our lives the moment we turn in faith to Him.*

A. W. Tozer

THE SELF-FULFILLING PROPHECY

May He grant you according to your heart's desire,
and fulfill all your purpose.

Psalm 20:4 NKJV

✴ The self-fulfilling prophecy is alive, well, and living at your house. If you trust God and have faith for the future, your optimistic beliefs will give you direction and motivation. That's one reason that you should never lose hope, but certainly not the only reason. The primary reason that you, as a believer, should never lose hope, is because of God's unfailing promises.

Make no mistake about it: thoughts are powerful things: your thoughts have the power to lift you up or to hold you down. When you acquire the habit of hopeful thinking, you will have acquired a powerful tool for improving your life. So if you fall into the habit of negative thinking, think again. After all, God's Word teaches us that Christ can overcome every difficulty (John 16:33). And when God makes a promise, He keeps it.

✴ *Hope looks for the good in people, opens doors for people, discovers what can be done to help, lights a candle, does not yield to cynicism. Hope sets people free.*

Barbara Johnson

✴ *Christ has turned all our sunsets into dawn.*

St. Clement of Alexandria

So Laugh!

A merry heart makes a cheerful countenance....

Proverbs 15:13 NKJV

❖ Barbara Johnson observes, "In our tense, uptight society where folks are rushing to make appointments they have already missed, a good laugh can be a refreshing as a cup of cold water in the desert." And she's right. Laughter is, indeed, God's gift, and He intends that we enjoy it. Yet sometimes, because of the inevitable stresses of everyday life, laughter seems only a distant memory.

As Christians, we have every reason to be cheerful and to be thankful. Our blessings from God are beyond measure, starting, of course, with a gift that is ours for the asking, God's gift of salvation through Christ Jesus.

Few things in life are more absurd than the sight of a grumpy Christian. So today, as you go about your daily activities, approach life with a grin and a chuckle. After all, God created laughter for a reason...to use it. So laugh!

❖ *I think everybody ought to be a laughing Christian. I'm convinced that there's just one place where there's not any laughter, and that's hell.*

Jerry Clower

WHERE IS YOUR TREASURE?

For where your treasure is, there your heart will be also.

Luke 12:34 NKJV

❀ In our demanding world, financial prosperity can be a good thing, but spiritual prosperity is profoundly more important. Certainly we all need the basic necessities of life, but once we meet those needs for our families and ourselves, the piling up of possessions creates more problems than it solves. Our real riches, of course, are not of this world. We are never really rich until we are rich in spirit. Yet we live in a society that leads us to believe otherwise. The media often glorifies material possessions above all else; God most certainly does not.

Martin Luther observed, "Many things I have tried to grasp and have lost. That which I have placed in God's hands I still have." His words apply to all of us. Our earthly riches are transitory; our spiritual riches, on the other hand, are everlasting.

Do you find yourself wrapped up in the concerns of the material world? If so, it's time to reorder your priorities and reassess your values . . . now!

❀ *It's sobering to contemplate how much time, effort, sacrifice, compromise, and attention we give to acquiring and increasing our supply of something that is totally insignificant in eternity.*

Anne Graham Lotz

WISDOM IN A DONUT SHOP

My cup runs over. Surely goodness and mercy shall
follow me all the days of my life; and I will dwell
in the house of the Lord Forever.

Psalm 23:5-6 NKJV

❈ Many years ago, this rhyme was posted on the wall of a small donut shop:

As you travel through life brother,
Whatever be your goal,
Keep your eye upon the donut,
And not upon the hole.

These simple words remind us of a profound truth: we should spend more time looking at the things we have, not worrying about the things we don't have.

When you think about it, you've got more blessings than you can count. So make it a habit to thank God for the gifts He's given you, not the gifts you wish He'd given you.

❈ *Other men see only a hopeless end, but the Christian rejoices in an endless hope.*

Gilbert M. Beeken

❈ *If you can't tell whether your glass is half-empty or half-full, you don't need another glass; what you need is better eyesight . . . and a more thankful heart.*

Marie T. Freeman

ALWAYS FORGIVING

Then Peter came to Him and said, "Lord, how often shall my brother sin against me, and I forgive him? Up to seven times?" Jesus said to him, "I do not say to you, up to seven times, but up to seventy times seven."

Matthew 18:21-22 NKJV

How often should we forgive other people? More times than we can count (Matthew 18:21-22). That's a tall order, but we must remember that it's an order from God—an order that must be obeyed.

In God's curriculum, forgiveness isn't optional; it's a required course. Sometimes, of course, we have a very difficult time forgiving the people who have hurt us, but if we don't find it in our hearts to forgive them, we not only hurt ourselves, we also disobey our Father in heaven. So we must forgive—and keep forgiving—as long as we live.

God gives us permission to forget our past and the understanding to live our present. He said He will remember our sins no more. (Psalm 103:11-12)

Serita Ann Jakes

What makes a Christian a Christian is not perfection but forgiveness.

Max Lucado

SOLVING PROBLEMS NOW

People who do what is right may have many problems,
but the Lord will solve them all.

Psalm 34:19 NCV

❋ The words of Psalm 34 remind us that the Lord solves problems for "people who do what is right." And usually, doing "what is right" means doing the uncomfortable work of confronting our problems sooner rather than later.

Life is an exercise in problem-solving. The question is not whether we will encounter problems; the real question is how we will choose to address them. When it comes to solving the problems of everyday living, we often know precisely what needs to be done, but we may be slow in doing it—especially if what needs to be done is difficult or uncomfortable for us. So we put off till tomorrow what should be done today.

So with no further ado, let the problem-solving begin . . . now.

❋ *What a comfort to know that God is present there in your life, available to meet every situation with you, that you are never left to face any problem alone.*

Vonette Bright

THE GREATEST AMONG US

So prepare your minds for service and have self-control.

1 Peter 1:13 NCV

❧ Jesus teaches that the most esteemed men and women are not the leaders of society or the captains of industry. To the contrary, Jesus teaches that the greatest among us are those who choose to minister and to serve.

Today, you may feel the temptation to build yourself up in the eyes of your neighbors. Resist that temptation. Instead, serve your neighbors quietly and without fanfare. Then, when you have done your best to serve your community and to serve your God, you can rest comfortably knowing that in the eyes of God you have achieved greatness. And God's eyes, after all, are the only ones that really count.

❧ *Service is the pathway to real significance.*

Rick Warren

❧ *We can love Jesus in the hungry, the naked, and the destitute who are dying...If you love, you will be willing to serve. And you will find Jesus in the distressing disguise of the poor.*

Mother Teresa

❧ *There is nothing small in the service of God.*

St. Francis of Sales

LIVING ABOVE THE CIRCUMSTANCES

In everything give thanks; for this is the will of
God in Christ Jesus for you.

1 Thessalonians 5:18 NKJV

❋ Have you thanked God today for blessings that are too numerous to count? Have you offered Him your heartfelt prayers and your wholehearted praise? If not, it's time slow down and to offer a prayer of thanksgiving to the One who has given you life on earth and life eternal.

The words of 1 Thessalonians 5:18 remind us to give thanks in every circumstance of life. But sometimes, when our hearts are troubled and our spirits are crushed, we don't feel like expressing gratitude. Yet even when the clouds of despair darken our lives, God offers us His love, His strength, and His Grace. And as believers, we must thank Him.

No matter our circumstances, we owe God so much more than we can ever repay, and the least we can do is to thank Him.

❋ *The act of thanksgiving is a demonstration of the fact that you are going to trust and believe God.*

Kay Arthur

❋ *The unthankful heart discovers no mercies; but the thankful heart will find, in every hour, some heavenly blessings!*

Henry Ward Beecher

BEYOND WORRY

Whoever listens to what is taught will succeed,
and whoever trusts the Lord will be happy.

Proverbs 16:20 NCV

❧ "Worry does not empty tomorrow of its sorrow; it empties today of its strength." So writes Corrie ten Boom, a woman who survived a Nazi concentration camp during World War II. And while our own situations cannot be compared to Corrie's, we still worry about countless matters both great and small. Even though we are Christians who have been given the assurance of salvation—even though we are Christians who have received the promise of God's love and protection—we find ourselves fretting over the countless details of everyday life. Jesus understood our concerns when he spoke the reassuring words found in Matthew 6: "So I tell you, don't worry . . . ." (NCV)

As you consider the promises of Jesus, remember that God still sits in His heaven and you are His beloved child. Then, perhaps, you will worry a little less and trust God a little more, and that's as it should be because God is trustworthy . . . and you are protected.

❧ *When times are tough, the Lord is our only security.*

Charles Swindoll

RIGHT OR WRONG?
THE CHOICE IS YOURS

*Light shines on those who do right; joy belongs to
those who are honest. Rejoice in the Lord,
you who do right. Praise his holy name.*

Psalm 97:11-12 NCV

❧ Everyday life is an adventure in decision-making.
Each day, we make countless decisions that hopefully
bring us closer to God. When we live according to
God's commandments, we share in His abundance
and His peace. But, when we turn our backs upon
God by disobeying Him, we bring needless suffering
upon ourselves and upon our families.

Do you seek God's peace and His blessings? Then
obey Him. When you're faced with a difficult choice
or a powerful temptation, seek God's counsel and
trust the counsel He gives. Invite God into your heart
and live according to His commandments. When
you do, you will be blessed today, and tomorrow, and
forever.

❧ *Have your heart right with Christ, and he will visit you
often, and so turn weekdays into Sundays, meals into
sacraments, homes into temples, and earth into heaven.*

C. H. Spurgeon

GOD'S INDESCRIBABLE GIFT

For God so loved the world that He gave His only
begotten Son, that whoever believes in Him
should not perish but have everlasting life.

John 3:16 NKJV

How much does God love you? To answer that question, you need only to look at the cross. God's love for you is so great that He sent His only Son to this earth to die for your sins and to offer you the priceless gift of eternal life.

You must decide whether or not to accept God's gift. Will you ignore it or embrace it? Will you return it or neglect it? Will you invite Christ to dwell in the center of your heart, or will you relegate Him to a position of lesser importance? The decision is yours, and so are the consequences. So choose wisely . . . and choose today.

The most profound essence of my nature is that I am capable of receiving God.

St. Augustine

Choose Jesus Christ! Deny yourself, take up the Cross, and follow Him—for the world must be shown. The world must see, in us, a discernible, visible, startling difference.

Elisabeth Elliot

THE WORLD . . . AND YOU

And do not be conformed to this world,
but be transformed by the renewing of your mind,
that you may prove what is that good and acceptable
and perfect will of God.

Romans 12:2 NKJV

✐ We live in the world, but we must not worship it. Our duty is to place God first and everything else second. But because we are fallible beings with imperfect faith, placing God in His rightful place is often difficult. In fact, at every turn, or so it seems, we are tempted to do otherwise.

The 21st Century world is a noisy, distracting place filled with countless opportunities to stray from God's will. The world seems to cry, "Worship me with your time, your money, your energy, and your thoughts!" But God commands otherwise: He commands us to worship Him and Him alone; everything else must be secondary.

✐ *The only ultimate disaster that can befall us, I have come to realize, is to feel ourselves to be home on earth.*

Max Lucado

✐ *I have a divided heart, trying to love God and the world at the same time. God says, "You can't love me as you should if you love this world too."*

Mary Morrison Suggs

BEHAVIOR THAT IS CONSISTENT WITH YOUR BELIEFS

Your beliefs about these things should be kept secret between you and God. People are happy if they can do what they think is right without feeling guilty.

Romans 14:22 NCV

⚘ Your beliefs shape your values, and your values shape your life. Is your life a clearly-crafted picture book of your creed? Are your actions always consistent with your beliefs? Are you willing to practice the philosophies that you preach? Hopefully so; otherwise, you'll be tormented by inconsistencies between your beliefs and your behaviors.

In describing our beliefs, our actions are far better descriptors than our words. Yet far too many of us spend more energy talking about our beliefs than living by them—with predictably poor results.

As believers, we must beware: Our actions should always give credence to the changes that Christ can make in the lives of those who choose to walk with Him.

⚘ *Believe and do what God says. The life-changing consequences will be limitless, and the results will be confidence and peace of mind.*

Franklin Graham

ACKNOWLEDGING YOUR BLESSINGS

The Lord bless you and keep you; The Lord make
His face shine upon you, And be gracious to you.

Numbers 6:24-25 NKJV

❧ Sometimes the demands of life leave us rushing from place to place with scarcely a moment to spare, and we may fail to pause and thank our Creator for His gifts. But, whenever we neglect to give proper thanks to the Father, we suffer because of our misplaced priorities.

Today, why not take a few minutes to begin making a list of your blessings? You most certainly will not be able to make a complete list, but you should jot down as many blessings as you can. When you do, you'll be amazed by God's gifts. He is, after all, the Giver of all good things. His love for you is eternal, as are His gifts. And it's never too soon—or too late—to offer Him thanks.

❧ *God's kindness is not like the sunset—brilliant in its intensity, but dying every second. God's generosity keeps coming and coming and coming.*

Bill Hybels

❧ *Oh! what a Savior, gracious to all, Oh! how His blessings round us fall, Gently to comfort, kindly to cheer, Sleeping or waking, God is near.*

Fanny Crosby

A PATTERN OF GOOD WORKS

*In all things showing yourself to be a pattern of good
works; in doctrine showing integrity,
reverence, incorruptibility . . . .*

Titus 2:7 NKJV

It has been said that character is what we are when
nobody is watching. How true. But, as Bill Hybels
correctly observed, "Every secret act of character,
conviction, and courage has been observed in living
color by our omniscient God." And isn't that a
sobering thought?

When we do things that we know aren't right, we
try to hide our misdeeds from family members and
friends. But even then, God is watching.

If you sincerely wish to walk with God, you
must seek, to the best of your ability, to follow His
commandments. When you do, your character will
take care of itself...and you won't need to look over
your shoulder to see who, besides God, is watching.

*There is something about having endured great loss that
brings purity of purpose and strength of character.*

Barbara Johnson

*Let God use times of waiting to mold and shape your
character. Let God use those times to purify you life and
make you into a clean vessel for His service.*

Henry Blackaby and Claude King

WHEN THE ANSWER IS NO

He heeded their prayer,
because they put their trust in him.

1 Chronicles 5:20 NKJV

❧ God answers our prayers. What God does not do is this: He does not always answer our prayers as soon as we might like, and He does not always answer our prayers by saying "Yes." God isn't an order-taker, and He's not some sort of cosmic vending machine. Sometimes—even when we want something very badly—our loving Heavenly Father responds to our requests by saying "No", and we must accept His answer, even if we don't understand it.

God answers prayers not only according to our wishes but also according to His master plan. We cannot know that plan, but we can know the Planner . . . and we must trust His wisdom, His righteousness, and His love. Always.

❧ *Let's never forget that some of God's greatest mercies are His refusals. He says no in order that He may, in some way we cannot imagine, say yes. All His ways with us are merciful. His meaning is always love.*

Elisabeth Elliot

❧ *Nothing is clearer than that prayer has its only worth and significance in the great fact that God hears and answers prayer.*

E. M. Bounds

BUILDING HIS CHURCH

For we are God's fellow workers; you are God's field,
you are God's building.

1 Corinthians 3:9 NKJV

❧ The church belongs to God; it is His just as certainly as we are His. When we help build God's church, we bear witness to the changes that He has made in our lives.

Today and every day, let us worship God with grateful hearts and helping hands as we support the church that He has created. Let us witness to our friends, to our families, and to the world. When we do so, we bless others—and we are blessed by the One who sent His Son to die so that we might have eternal life.

❧ *The church needs the power and the gifts of the Holy Spirit more now than ever before.*

Corrie ten Boom

❧ *Only participation in the full life of a local church builds spiritual muscle.*

Rick Warren

❧ *The church is where it's at. The first place of Christian service for any Christian is in a local church.*

Jerry Clower

ANOTHER OPPORTUNITY

*When we were baptized, we were buried with Christ
and shared his death. So, just as Christ was raised
from the dead by the wonderful power of the Father,
we also can live a new life.*

Romans 6:4 NCV

❧ Each morning offers a fresh opportunity to invite
Christ, yet once again, to rule over our hearts and our
days. Each morning presents yet another opportunity
to take up His cross and follow in His footsteps.

God's Word is clear: When we genuinely invite
Him to reign over our hearts, and when we accept His
transforming love, we are forever changed. When we
welcome Christ into our hearts, an old life ends and a
new way of living—along with a completely new way
of viewing the world—begins.

Today, let us rejoice in the new life that is ours
through Christ, and let us follow Him, step by step,
on the path that He first walked.

❧ *God specializes in things fresh and firsthand. His
plans for you this year may outshine those of the past.
He's prepared to fill your days with reasons to give Him
praise.*

Joni Eareckson Tada

THE SOURCE OF COURAGE AND HOPE

Give your worries to the Lord, and he will take care of you. He will never let good people down.

Psalm 55:22 NCV

Even dedicated followers of Jesus may find their courage tested by the inevitable anxieties and fears that beset even the most courageous Christians.

When you find yourself worried about the challenges of today or the uncertainties of tomorrow, you must ask yourself whether or not you are ready to place your concerns and your life in God's all-powerful, all-knowing, all-loving hands. If the answer to that question is yes—as it should be—then you can draw courage and hope from the source of strength that never fails: your Heavenly Father.

Seeing that a Pilot steers the ship in which we sail, who will never allow us to perish even in the midst of shipwrecks, there is no reason why our minds should be overwhelmed with fear and overcome with weariness.

John Calvin

Just as courage is faith in good, so discouragement is faith in evil, and, while courage opens the door to good, discouragement opens it to evil.

Hannah Whitall Smith

Defeating Discouragement

The Lord himself will go before you.
He will be with you; he will not leave you or forget you.
Don't be afraid and don't worry.

Deuteronomy 31:8 NCV

❧ When we fail to meet the expectations of others (or, for that matter, the expectations that we have set for ourselves), we may be tempted to abandon hope. Thankfully, on those cloudy days when our strength is sapped and our faith is shaken, there exists a source from which we can draw courage and wisdom. That source is God.

When we seek to form a more intimate and dynamic relationship with our Creator, He renews our spirits and restores our souls. God's promise is made clear in Isaiah 40:31: "But those who wait on the Lord shall renew their strength; They shall mount up with wings like eagles, They shall run and not be weary, They shall walk and not faint" (NKJV). And upon this promise we can—and should—depend.

❧ *Faith and discouragement are opposites. Faith is taking God at His Word no matter how bleak the circumstances appear to be. Discouragement is focusing on distressing circumstances in spite of what God has said. Learn to trust God.*

Jerry Falwell

WHEN IT'S HARD TO BE KIND

Do not be interested only in your own life,
but be interested in the lives of others.

Philippians 2:4 NCV

❧ When we feel happy or generous, we find it easy to be kind. Other times, when we are discouraged or tired, we can scarcely summon the energy to utter a single kind word. But, God's commandment is clear: He intends that we make the conscious choice to treat others with kindness and respect, no matter our circumstances, no matter our emotions.

Today, as you consider all the things that Christ has done in your life, honor Him by following His commandment and obeying the Golden Rule. He expects no less, and He deserves no less.

❧ *The Golden Rule starts at home, but it should never stop there.*

Marie T. Freeman

❧ *Anything done for another is done for oneself.*

Pope John Paul II

❧ *Reach out and care for someone who needs the touch of hospitality. The time you spend caring today will be a love gift that will blossom into the fresh joy of God's Spirit in the future.*

Emilie Barnes

A Promise You Can Count On

Blessed is the man who endures temptation;
for when he has been approved, he will receive
the crown of life which the Lord has promised
to those who love Him.

James 1:12 NKJV

❧ Throughout the seasons of life, we must all endure life-altering personal losses that leave us breathless. When we do, we may be overwhelmed by fear, by doubt, or by both. Thankfully, God has promised that He will never desert us. And God keeps His promises.

Life is often challenging, but as Christians, we must trust the promises of our Heavenly Father. God loves us, and He will protect us. In times of hardship, He will comfort us; in times of sorrow, He will dry our tears. When we are troubled, or weak, or sorrowful, God is with us. His love endures, not only for today, but also for all of eternity.

❧ *Teach us to set our hopes on heaven, to hold firmly to the promise of eternal life, so that we can withstand the struggles and storms of this world.*

Max Lucado

HOPE FOR TROUBLED TIMES

*They won't be afraid of bad news; their hearts are
steady because they trust the Lord.*

Psalm 112:7 NCV

❧ These are troubled times, times when we have
legitimate fears for the future of our nation, our world,
and our families. We live in a fear-based world, a
world where bad news travels at light speed and good
news doesn't. But as Christians, we have every reason
to live courageously. After all, the ultimate battle has
already been fought and won on that faraway cross at
Calvary.

Perhaps you, like countless other believers, have
found your courage tested by the anxieties and fears
that are an inevitable part of 21st-Century life. If so,
God wants to have a little chat with you. When you
find your courage tested to the breaking point, God
wants to remind you that He is not just near, He is
here.

Your Heavenly Father is your Protector and your
Deliverer. Call upon Him in your hour of need, and
be comforted. Whatever your challenge, whatever
your trouble, God can certainly handle it. And will.

❧ *God shields us from most of the things we fear, but
when He chooses not to shield us, He unfailingly allots
grace in the measure needed.*

Elisabeth Elliot

YOUR BODY, GOD'S TEMPLE

*Don't you know that you are God's temple and that
God's Spirit lives in you?*

1 Corinthians 3:16 NCV

✎ Physical fitness is a choice, a choice that requires discipline—it's as simple as that. Are you shaping up or spreading out?

Do you eat sensibly and exercise regularly, or do you spend most of your time on the couch with a snack in one hand and a clicker in the other? Are you choosing to treat your body like a temple or a trash heap? How you answer these questions will help determine how long you live and how well you live.

So, do yourself this favor: treat your body like a one-of-a-kind gift from God . . . because that's precisely what your body is.

✎ *Exercise and physical fitness have a cause-and-effect relationship; fitness comes as a direct result of regular, sustained, and intense exercise.*

Jim Maxwell

✎ *Maximum physical health happens when the body—with all its chemicals, parts, and systems—is functioning as closely to the way God designed it to function.*

Dr. Walt Larimore

YOUR WAY OR GOD'S WAY

A man's heart plans his way,
but the Lord directs his steps.

Proverbs 16:9 NKJV

❧ The popular song "My Way" is a perfectly good tune, but it's not a perfect guide for life. If you're looking for life's perfect prescription, you'd better forget about doing things your way and start doing things God's way. The most important decision of your life is, of course, your commitment to accept Jesus Christ as your personal Lord and Savior. And once your eternal destiny is secured, you will undoubtedly ask yourself the question "What now, Lord?" If you earnestly seek God's will for your life, you will find it…in time.

Sometimes, God's plans are crystal clear; sometimes they are not. So be patient, keep searching, and keep praying. If you do, then in time, God will answer your prayers and make His plans known. You'll discover those plans by doing things His way . . . and you'll be eternally grateful that you did.

❧ *Ours is an intentional God, brimming over with motive and mission. He never does things capriciously or decides with the flip of a coin.*

Joni Eareckson Tada

GREAT IS THY FAITHFULNESS

*God is faithful, by whom you were called into
the fellowship of His Son, Jesus Christ our Lord.*

1 Corinthians 1:9 NKJV

⚘ As the hymn writer so eloquently wrote of God, "Great is Thy Faithfulness." God is faithful to us even when we are not faithful to Him. God keeps His promises to us even when we stray far from His will. He continues to love us even when we disobey His commandments. But God does not force His blessings upon us. If we are to experience His love and His grace, we must claim them for ourselves.

Are you tired, discouraged or fearful? Be comforted: God is with you. Are you confused? Listen to the quiet voice of your Heavenly Father. Are you bitter? Talk with God and seek His guidance. Are you celebrating a great victory? Thank God and praise Him. He is the Giver of all things good. In whatever condition you find yourself, trust God and be comforted. The Father is with you now and forever.

⚘ *God's faithfulness has never depended on the faithfulness of his children…. God is greater than our weakness. In fact, I think, it is our weakness that reveals how great God is.*

Max Lucado

GOD'S GUIDANCE

Those whom the Lord blesses will inherit the land . . . .

Psalms 37:22 NCV

❧ God is intensely interested in each of us, and He will guide our steps if we serve Him obediently.

When we sincerely offer heartfelt prayers to our Heavenly Father, He will give direction and meaning to our lives—but He won't force us to follow Him. To the contrary, God has given us the free will to follow His commandments . . . or not.

When we stray from God's commandments, we invite bitter consequences. But, when we follow His commandments, and when we genuinely and humbly seek His will, He touches our hearts and leads us on the path of His choosing.

Will you trust God to guide your steps? You should. When you entrust your life to Him completely and without reservation, God will give you the strength to meet any challenge, the courage to face any trial, and the wisdom to live in His righteousness and in His peace. So trust Him today and seek His guidance. When you do, your next step will be the right one.

❧ *God's leading will never be contrary to His word.*

Vonette Bright

CONTENTED IN HIM

The LORD will give strength to His people;
The LORD will bless His people with peace.

Psalm 29:11 NKJV

❧ Everywhere we turn, or so it seems, the world promises us contentment and happiness. We are bombarded by messages offering us the "good life" if only we will purchase products and services that are designed to provide happiness, success, and contentment. But the contentment that the world offers is fleeting and incomplete. Thankfully, the contentment that God offers is all encompassing and everlasting.

Do you sincerely want to be a contented Christian? Then set your mind and your heart upon God's love and His grace. Seek first the salvation that is available through a personal relationship with Jesus Christ, and then claim the joy, the contentment, and the spiritual abundance that God offers His children.

❧ *The secret of contentment in the midst of change is found in having roots in the changeless Christ—the same yesterday, today and forever.*

Ed Young

❧ *We will never be happy until we make God the source of our fulfillment and the answer to our longings.*

Stormie Omartian

PERFECT WISDOM

Therefore whoever hears these sayings of Mine,
and does them, I will liken him to a wise man who built
his house on the rock: and the rain descended, the floods
came, and the winds blew and beat on that house;
and it did not fall, for it was founded on the rock.

Matthew 7:24-25 NKJV

❦ Where will you place your trust today? Will you trust in the wisdom of fallible men and women, or will you place your faith God's perfect wisdom? Where you choose to place your trust will determine will determine the direction and quality of your life.

Are you tired? Discouraged? Fearful? Be comforted and trust God. Are you worried or anxious? Be confident in God's power and trust His Holy Word. Are you confused? Listen to the quiet voice of your Heavenly Father. He is not a God of confusion. Talk with Him; listen to Him; trust Him. He is steadfast, and He is your protector . . .forever.

❦ *God Himself is what enlightens understanding about everything else in life. Knowledge about any subject is fragmentary without the enlightenment that comes from His relationship to it.*

Beth Moore

HAPPINESS AND HOLINESS

Happy are the people who live at your Temple . . . .
Happy are those whose strength comes from you.

Psalm 84:4-5 NKJV

❧ The happiest people are not those who rebel against God; the happiest people are those who love God and obey His commandments. Do you seek happiness, abundance, and contentment? If so, here are some things you should do: Love God and His Son; depend upon God for strength; try, to the best of your abilities, to follow God's will; and strive to obey His Holy Word. When you do these things, you'll discover that happiness goes hand-in-hand with righteousness.

What does life have in store for you? A world full of possibilities (of course it's up to you to seize them), and God's promise of abundance (of course it's up to you to accept it). Your Creator has blessed you beyond measure. Honor Him with your prayers, your words, your deeds, and your joy.

❧ *Christ is the secret, the source, the substance, the center, and the circumference of all true and lasting gladness.*

Mrs. Charles E. Cowman

❧ *To be in a state of true grace is to be miserable no more; it is to be happy forever. A soul in this state is a soul near and dear to God. It is a soul housed in God.*

Thomas Brooks

TO GOD BE THE GLORY

*God is against the proud,
but he gives grace to the humble.*

1 Peter 5:5 NCV

❧ Reality breeds humility. Dietrich Bonhoeffer observed, "It is very easy to overestimate the importance of our own achievements in comparison with what we owe others." And he was right.

As Christians, we have a profound reason to be humble: We have been refashioned and saved by Jesus Christ, and that salvation came not because of our own good works but because of God's grace. Thus, we are not "self-made," we are "God-made," and "Christ-saved." How, then, can we be boastful?

So, instead of puffing out your chest and saying, "Look how wonderful I am," give credit where credit is due, starting with God. And, rest assured: There is no such thing as a self-made man or woman. All of us are made by God…and He deserves the glory, not us.

❧ *Without humility of heart all the other virtues by which one runs toward God seem—and are—absolutely worthless.*

Angela of Foligno

❧ *A humble heart is like a magnet that draws the favor of God toward us.*

Jim Cymbala

Beyond Envy

*Therefore, laying aside all malice, all deceit, hypocrisy,
envy, and all evil speaking, as newborn babes, desire
the pure milk of the word, that you may grow thereby.*

1 Peter 2:1-2 NKJV

❧ God's Word warns us that envy is sin. Thus, we
must guard ourselves against the natural tendency
to feel resentment and jealousy when other people
experience good fortune. As believers, we have
absolutely no reason to be envious of any people
on earth. After all, as Christians we are already
recipients of the greatest gift in all creation: God's
grace. We have been promised the gift of eternal life
through God's only begotten Son, and we must count
that gift as our most precious possession.

So here's a simple suggestion that is guaranteed
to bring you happiness: fill your heart with God's
love, God's promises, and God's Son . . . and when
you do so, leave no room for envy, hatred, bitterness,
or regret.

❧ *How can you possess the miseries of envy when you
possess in Christ the best of all portions?*

C. H. Spurgeon

❧ *What God asks, does, or requires of others is not my
business; it is His.*

Kay Arthur

YOUR SPIRITUAL JOURNEY

And I pray that you and all God's holy people will have the power to understand the greatness of Christ's love—how wide and how long and how high and how deep that love is. Christ's love is greater than anyone can ever know, but I pray that you will be able to know that love. Then you can be filled with the fullness of God.

Ephesians 3:18–19 NCV

❦ The journey toward spiritual maturity lasts a lifetime. As Christians, we can and should continue to grow in the love and the knowledge of our Savior as long as we live. When we cease to grow, either emotionally or spiritually, we do ourselves a profound disservice. But, if we study God's Word, if we obey His commandments, and if we live in the center of His will, we will not be "stagnant" believers; we will, instead, be healthy, growing Christians.

Each day, we make countless decisions that can bring us closer to God . . . or not. When we live according to the principles contained in God's Holy Word, we embark upon a journey of spiritual maturity that results in life abundant and life eternal.

❦ *Being a Christian means accepting the terms of creation, accepting God as our maker and redeemer, and growing day by day into an increasingly glorious creature in Christ.*

Eugene Peterson

A PASSIONATE LIFE

*Do not be lazy but work hard, serving the Lord
with all your heart.*

Romans 12:11 NCV

Are you passionate about your life, your loved ones, your work, and your faith? As a believer who has been saved by a risen Christ, you should be.

As a thoughtful Christian, you have every reason to be enthusiastic about life, but sometimes the inevitable struggles of life may cause you to feel decidedly unenthusiastic. If you feel that your enthusiasm is slowly fading away, it's time to slow down, to rest, to count your blessings, and to pray. When you feel worried or weary, you must pray fervently for God to renew your sense of wonderment and excitement.

Life with God is a glorious adventure; revel in it. When you do, God will most certainly smile upon your work and your life.

Exploring the desire of our hearts is not a waste of time. It is precisely the place where God is stirring.

Paula Rinehart

I do not want merely to possess a faith; I want a faith that possesses me.

Charles Kingsley

PLEASING GOD

Our only goal is to please God whether we live here or there, because we must all stand before Christ to be judged.

2 Corinthians 5:9-10 NCV

❧ Sometimes you may become so wrapped up in meeting society's expectations that you fail to focus on God's expectations. When God made you, he equipped you with an array of talents and abilities that are uniquely yours. It's up to you to discover those talents and to use them, but sometimes the world will encourage you to do otherwise. At times, society will attempt to cubbyhole you, to standardize you, and to make you fit into particular, preformed mold. God has other plans.

Instead, seek God's guidance as you focus your energies on becoming the best "you" that you can possibly be. And, when it comes to matters of conscience, seek approval not from your peers, but from your Creator.

Your primary obligation is not to please imperfect men and women. Your obligation is to strive diligently to meet the expectations of an all-knowing and perfect God. Trust Him always. Love Him always. Praise Him always. And seek to please Him. Always.

❧ *You must never sacrifice your relationship with God for the sake of a relationship with another person.*

Charles Stanley

DOING IT NOW

*Let us walk properly, as in the day,
not in revelry and drunkenness, not in lewdness and lust,
not in strife and envy.*

Romans 13:13 NKJV

❧ Procrastination is, at its core, a struggle against oneself; the only antidote is action. The habit of procrastination takes a two-fold toll on its victims. First, important work goes unfinished; second (and more importantly), valuable energy is wasted in the process of putting off the things that remain undone. Procrastination results from an individual's short-sighted attempt to postpone temporary discomfort. What results is a senseless cycle of 1. delay, followed by 2. worry followed by 3. a panicky and often futile attempt to "catch up."

Once you acquire the habit of doing what needs to be done when it needs to be done, you will avoid untold trouble, worry, and stress. So learn to defeat procrastination by paying less attention to your fears and more attention to your responsibilities. God has created a world that punishes procrastinators and rewards men who "do it now." Life doesn't procrastinate—neither should you.

❧ *Don't duck the most difficult problems. That just insures that the hardest part will be left when you're most tired. Get the big one done, and it's all downhill from then on.*

Norman Vincent Peale

LIVING IN CHRIST'S LOVE

Yes, my dear children, live in him so that when Christ comes back, we can be without fear and not be ashamed in his presence. If you know that Christ is all that is right, you know that all who do right are God's children.

1 John 2:28–29 NCV

❧ God's love for us is unconditional. No matter what we have done good or bad God's love is steady and sure. Even though we are imperfect, fallible human beings, even though we have fallen far short of God's commandments, Christ loves us still. His love is perfect; it does not waver—it does not change. Our task, as believers, is to accept Christ's love and to encourage others to do likewise.

In today's troubled world, we all need the love and the peace that is found through the Son of God. Thankfully, Christ's love has no limits. We, in turn, should love Him with no limits, beginning now and ending never.

❧ *We are the earthen vessels, the jars of clay, that bring the life and love of Christ to one another.*

Sheila Walsh

❧ *The richest meaning of your life is contained in the idea that Christ loved you enough to give His life for you.*

Calvin Miller

MEANINGFUL MEDITATION

Finally, brethren, whatever things are true,
whatever things are noble, whatever things are just,
whatever things are pure, whatever things are lovely,
whatever things are of good report, if there is any virtue
and if there is anything praiseworthy—
meditate on these things.

Philippians 4:8 NKJV

🕊 How will you direct your thoughts today? Will you obey the words of Philippians 4:8 by dwelling upon those things that are honorable, true, and worthy of praise? Or will you allow your thoughts to be hijacked by the negativity that seems to dominate our troubled world?

Are you fearful, angry, bored, or worried? Are you so preoccupied with the concerns of this day that you fail to thank God for the promise of eternity? Are you confused, bitter, or pessimistic? If so, God wants to have a little talk with you. He wants to remind you of His infinite love and His boundless grace. As you contemplate these things, and as you give thanks for God's blessings, negativity should no longer dominate your day or your life.

🕊 *People who do not develop and practice good thinking often find themselves at the mercy of their circumstances.*

John Maxwell

YOU ARE PROTECTED

The Lord himself will go before you.
He will be with you; he will not leave you or forget you.
Don't be afraid and don't worry.

Deuteronomy 31:8 NCV

❧ The Bible makes this promise: God will care for you and protect you. In the 6th Chapter of Matthew, Jesus made this point clear when He said,

Do not worry about your life, what you will eat or what you will drink; nor about your body, what you will put on. Is not life more than food and the body more than clothing? Look at the birds of the air, for they neither sow nor reap nor gather into barns; yet your heavenly Father feeds them. Are you not of more value than they? Which of you by worrying can add one cubit to his stature? . . . Therefore do not worry about tomorrow, for tomorrow will worry about its own things. Sufficient for the day is its own trouble (25-27, 34 NKJV).

This beautiful passage reminds you that God still sits in His heaven and you are His beloved child. Simply put, you are protected.

❧ *The Lord God of heaven and earth, the Almighty Creator of all things, He who holds the universe in His hand as though it were a very little thing, He is your Shepherd, and He has charged Himself with the care and keeping of you, as a shepherd is charged with the care and keeping of his sheep.*

Hannah Whitall Smith

OUR CIRCLE

Do not be unequally yoked together with unbelievers.
For what fellowship has righteousness with lawlessness?
And what communion has light with darkness?

2 Corinthians 6:14 NKJV

❧ As we travel along life's road, we build lifelong relationships with a small, dear circle of family and friends. And how best do we build and maintain these relationships? By following the Word of God. Healthy relationships are built upon honesty, compassion, responsible behavior, trust, and optimism. Healthy relationships are built upon the Golden Rule. Healthy relationships are built upon sharing and caring. All of these principles are found time and time again in God's Holy Word. When we read God's Word and follow His commandments, we enrich our own lives and the lives of those who are closest to us.

❧ *Line by line, moment by moment, special times are etched into our memories in the permanent ink of everlasting love in our relationships.*

Gloria Gaither

❧ *A friend who loves will be more concerned about what is best for you than being accepted by you.*

Charles Stanley

FACE-TO-FACE WITH OLD MAN TROUBLE

*When you pass through the waters, I will be
with you; and through the rivers, they shall not
overflow you. When you walk through the fire,
you shall not be burned, nor shall the flame scorch you.
For I am the Lord your God,
The Holy One of Israel, your Savior.*

Isaiah 43:2-3 NKJV

❧ As life unfolds, all of us encounter occasional setbacks: Those occasional visits from Old Man Trouble are simply a fact of life, and none of us are exempt. When tough times arrive, we may be forced to rearrange our plans and our priorities. But even on our darkest days, we must remember that God's love remains constant.

The fact that we encounter adversity is not nearly so important as the way we choose to deal with it. When tough times arrive, we have a clear choice: we can begin the difficult work of tackling our troubles . . . or not. When we summon the courage to look Old Man Trouble squarely in the eye, an amazing thing usually happens: he blinks.

❧ *Faith is a strong power, mastering any difficulty in the strength of the Lord who made heaven and earth.*

Corrie ten Boom

A PRESCRIPTION FOR PANIC

Anxiety in the heart of man causes depression,
but a good word makes it glad.

Proverbs 12:25 NKJV

❧ We live in a world that sometimes seems to shift beneath our feet. We live in an uncertain world, a world where tragedies can befall even the most godly among us. And we are members of an anxious society, a society in which the changes we face threaten to outpace our abilities to make adjustments. No wonder we sometimes find ourselves beset by feelings of anxiety and panic.

At times, our anxieties may stem from physical causes—chemical imbalances in the brain that result in severe emotional distress or relentless panic attacks. In such cases, modern medicine offers hope to those who suffer. But oftentimes, our anxieties result from spiritual deficits, not physical ones. And when we're spiritually depleted, the best prescription is found not in the medicine cabinet but deep inside the human heart. What we need is a higher daily dose of God's love, God's peace, God's assurance, and God's presence. And how do we acquire these blessings from our Creator? Through prayer, through meditation, through worship, and through trust.

❧ *The thing that preserves a man from panic is his relationship to God.*

Oswald Chambers

BEHAVIOR REFLECTS BELIEF

*As you have therefore received Christ Jesus the Lord,
so walk in Him, rooted and built up in Him
and established in the faith, as you have been taught,
abounding in it with thanksgiving.*

Colossians 2:6-7 NKJV

❧ St. Francis of Assisi stated, "Preach the gospel everyday; if necessary, use words." And his advice still stands. As Christians, we must do our best to make sure that our actions are accurate reflections of our beliefs. Our theology must be demonstrated, not only by our words but, more importantly, by our actions. In short, we should be practical believers, quick to act whenever we see an opportunity to serve God.

English clergyman Thomas Fuller observed, "He does not believe who does not live according to his beliefs." These words are most certainly true. We may proclaim our beliefs to our hearts' content, but our proclamations will mean nothing—to others or to ourselves—unless we accompany our words with deeds that match. The sermons that we live are far more compelling than the ones we preach.

❧ *Study the Bible and observe how the persons behaved and how God dealt with them. There is explicit teaching on every condition of life.*

Corrie ten Boom

CELEBRATION NOW

Sing a new song to him; play well and joyfully.

Psalm 33:3 NCV

❧ Life should never be taken for granted. Not only should we whistle while we work, we should also celebrate each day we live. Every day is a priceless gift from God and should be treated as such.

Hannah Whitall Smith observed, "How changed our lives would be if we could only fly through the days on wings of surrender and trust!" And Clement of Alexandria noted, "All our life is a celebration for us; we are convinced, in fact, that God is always everywhere. We sing while we work…we pray while we carry out all life's other occupations." These words remind us that this day is God's creation, a gift to be treasured and savored.

Today, let us celebrate life with smiles on our faces and kind words on our lips. After all, this is God's day, and He has given us clear instructions for its use. We are commanded to rejoice and be glad.

❧ *The people whom I have seen succeed best in life have always been cheerful and hopeful people who went about their business with smiles on their faces.*

Charles Kingsley

A SACRIFICIAL LOVE

I am the good shepherd.
The good shepherd gives His life for the sheep.

John 10:11 NKJV

🕊 Christ's love is perfect and steadfast. Even though we are fallible and wayward, the Shepherd cares for us still. Even though we have fallen far short of the Father's commandments, Christ loves us with a power and depth that is beyond our understanding. The sacrifice that Jesus made upon the cross was made for each of us, and His love endures to the edge of eternity and beyond.

Christ's love changes everything. When you accept His gift of grace, you are transformed, not only for today, but also for all eternity. If you haven't already done so, accept Jesus Christ as your Savior. He's waiting patiently for you to invite Him into your heart. Please don't make Him wait a single minute longer.

🕊 *This hard place in which you perhaps find yourself is the very place in which God is giving you opportunity to look only to Him, to spend time in prayer, and to learn long-suffering, gentleness, meekness—in short, to learn the depths of the love that Christ Himself has poured out on all of us.*

Elisabeth Elliot

REAL REPENTANCE

They should repent, turn to God,
and do works befitting repentance.

Acts 26:20 NKJV

❦ Who among us has sinned? All of us. But the good news is this: When we do ask God's forgiveness and turn our hearts to Him, He forgives us absolutely and completely.

Genuine repentance requires more than simply offering God apologies for our misdeeds. Real repentance may start with feelings of sorrow and remorse, but it ends only when we turn away from the sin that has heretofore distanced us from our Creator. In truth, we offer our most meaningful apologies to God, not with our words, but with our actions. As long as we are still engaged in sin, we may be "repenting," but we have not fully "repented." So, if there is an aspect of your life that is distancing you from your God, ask for His forgiveness, and—just as importantly—stop sinning. Now.

❦ *Repentance involves a radical change of heart and mind in which we agree with God's evaluation of our sin and then take specific action to align ourselves with His will.*

Henry Blackaby

FEEDING THE CHURCH

God put everything under his power and made him
the head over everything for the church, which is
Christ's body. The church is filled with Christ,
and Christ fills everything in every way.

Ephesians 1:22-23 NCV

To know God is to grow closer to Him. And one of the most important ways we can grow closer to God is to be involved in His church.

In the Book of Acts, Luke reminds us to "feed the church of God" (20:28). As Christians who have been saved by a loving, compassionate Creator, we are compelled not only to worship Him in our hearts but also to worship Him in the presence of fellow believers.

Do you feed the church of God? Do you attend regularly, and are you an active participant? The answer to these questions will have a profound impact on the quality and direction of your spiritual journey.

So do yourself a favor: become actively involved in your church. Don't just go to church out of habit. Go to church out of a sincere desire to know and worship God. When you do, you'll be blessed by the One who sent His Son to die so that you might have everlasting life.

Man was created by God to know and love Him in a permanent, personal relationship.

Anne Graham Lotz

ALWAYS PROTECTED

*Be of good courage, And He shall strengthen your heart,
All you who hope in the Lord.*

Psalm 31:24 NKJV

❧ Being a courageous believer in this day and age is no easy task. Ours is a time of uncertainty and danger, a time when even the most courageous among us have legitimate cause for concern.

But here's the good news: if you've turned your heart and your life over to Jesus, you can live courageously, knowing that you have been saved by a loving Father and His only begotten Son.

Today, promise yourself that you will live without fear, knowing that even in these troubled times, God is always as near as your next breath—and you are always protected.

❧ *God did away with all my fear. It was time for someone to stand up—or in my case, sit down. So I refused to move.*

Rosa Parks

❧ *A man who is intimate with God will never be intimidated by men.*

Leonard Ravenhill

❧ *Call upon God. Prayer itself can defuse fear.*

Bill Hybels

NOT ENOUGH HOURS?

It is good to give thanks to the Lord,
And to sing praises to Your name, O Most High;
To declare Your lovingkindness in the morning,
And Your faithfulness every night.

Psalms 92:1-2 NKJV

❧ Each day has 1,440 minutes—do you value your relationship with God enough to spend a few of those minutes with Him? He deserves that much of your time and more—is He receiving it from you? Hopefully so. But if you find that you're simply "too busy" for a daily chat with your Father in heaven, it's time to take a long, hard look at your priorities and your values.

As you consider your plans for the day ahead, here's a tip: organize your life around this simple principle: "God first." When you place your Creator where He belongs—at the very center of your day and your life—the rest of your priorities will fall into place.

❧ *Knowing God involves an intimate, personal relationship that is developed over time through prayer and getting answers to prayer, through Bible study and applying its teaching to our lives, through obedience and experiencing the power of God, through moment-by-moment submission to Him that results in a moment-by-moment filling of the Holy Spirit.*

Anne Graham Lotz

FINDING ENCOURAGEMENT

*Don't be afraid, because the Lord your God
will be with you everywhere you go.*

Joshua 1:9 NCV

⇥ Are you a hopeful, optimistic Christian who associates with like-minded people? If so, then you're both wise and blessed.

God offers us the strength to meet our challenges, and He offers us hope for the future. One way that He shares His message of hope is through the words of encouraging friends and family members.

Hope, like other human emotions, is contagious. If we associate with hope-filled, enthusiastic people, their enthusiasm will have a tendency to lift our spirits. But if we find ourselves spending too much time in the company of naysayers, pessimists, or cynics, our thoughts—like the naysayers'—will tend to be negative.

So do yourself a favor by spending time with hope-filled people. And, when you catch their enthusiasm, share a little of that hope with those who need it.

⇥ *I was learning something important: we are most vulnerable to the piercing winds of doubt when we distance ourselves from the mission and fellowship to which Christ has called us. Our night of discouragement will seem endless and our task impossible, unless we recognize that He stands in our midst.*

Joni Eareckson Tada

ENERGIZED FOR LIFE

*Therefore, my beloved, as you have always obeyed,
not as in my presence only, but now much more in
my absence, work out your own salvation with fear
and trembling; for it is God who works in you both
to will and to do for His good pleasure.*

Philippians 2:12-13 NKJV

⊰ Are you fired with enthusiasm for Christ? If so,
congratulations, and keep up the good work! But, if
your spiritual batteries are running low, then perhaps
you're spending too much energy working for yourself
and not enough energy working for God.

If you're feeling tired, or troubled, or both, don't
despair. Instead, seek strength from the source that
never fails; that source, of course, is your Heavenly
Father. And rest assured—when you sincerely
petition Him, He will give you all the strength you
need to live victoriously for Him.

⊰ God doesn't camouflage the old; he restores the new.
The Master Builder will pull out the original plan and
restore it. He will restore the vigor, he will restore the
energy. He will restore the hope. He will restore the soul.

Max Lucado

⊰ In her heart of hearts, a woman draws her emotional
strength, and sometimes even her physical energy, from
her relationships.

Dianna Booher

WHAT KIND OF EXAMPLE?

In every way be an example of doing good deeds.
When you teach, do it with honesty and seriousness.

Titus 2:7 NCV

❧ Are you the kind of Christian whose life serves as a powerful example of decency and morality? Are you a person whose behavior serves as a positive role model for others? Are you the kind of believer whose actions, day in and day out, are based upon integrity, fidelity, and a love for the Lord? If so, you are not only blessed by God, you are also a powerful force for good in a world that desperately needs positive influences such as yours.

William J. Toms advised, "Be careful how you live. You may be the only Bible someone ever reads." And that's sound advice because our families and friends are watching . . . and so, for that matter, is God.

❧ *A holy life will produce the deepest impression. Lighthouses blow no horns; they only shine.*

D. L. Moody

❧ *We are to leave an impression on all those we meet that communicates whose we are and what kingdom we represent.*

Lisa Bevere

QUALITY TIME

*So teach us to number our days, that we may gain
a heart of wisdom.*

Psalm 90:12 NKJV

❧ When it comes to spending time with your family,
you've probably heard about "quality time" and
"quantity time." Your family needs both. You should
spend lots of time with your family, and the time you
spend with them should have a heaping helping of
meaningful moments.

If you're lucky enough to be a parent, remember
this: Parenting is a full-time job; it is a lifetime
commitment with great responsibilities and the
potential for even greater rewards. Your challenge, of
course, is to raise your children lovingly, responsibly,
and according to God's commandments. When you
do, the difficult job of parenting is made easier, and
your family will be forever blessed.

While caring for your clan, you should do your best
to ensure that God remains squarely at the center of
your household. When you do, God will bless you and
yours in ways that you could have scarcely imagined.

❧ *There is so much compassion and understanding that
is gained when we've experienced God's grace firsthand
within our own families.*

Lisa Whelchel

In Focus

Keep your eyes focused on what is right, and look straight ahead to what is good. Be careful what you do, and always do what is right. Don't turn off the road of goodness; keep away from evil paths.

Proverbs 4:25-27 NCV

᪥ Are you willing to focus your thoughts and energies on God's blessings and upon His will for your life? Or will you turn your thoughts to other things? This day—and every day hereafter—is a chance to celebrate the life that God has given you. It's also a chance to give thanks to the One who has offered you more blessings than you can possibly count.

Today, why not focus your thoughts on the joy that is rightfully yours in Christ? Why not take time to celebrate God's glorious creation? Why not trust your hopes instead of your fears? When you do, you will think optimistically about yourself and your world . . . and you can then share your optimism with others. They'll be better for it, and so will you. But not necessarily in that order.

᪥ *When Jesus is in our midst, he brings His limitless power along as well. But, Jesus must be in the middle, all eyes and hearts focused on Him.*

Shirley Dobson

᪥ *Whatever we focus on determines what we become.*

E. Stanley Jones

A LIFE OF FULFILLMENT

For You, O God, have tested us; You have refined us as silver is refined . . . we went through fire and through water; but You brought us out to rich fulfillment.

Psalm 66:10–12 NKJV

❪ Sometimes, amid the inevitable hustle and bustle of daily life, we can forfeit—albeit temporarily—the joy of Christ as we wrestle with the challenges of daily living. Everywhere we turn, or so it seems, the world promises fulfillment, contentment, and happiness. But the contentment that the world offers is fleeting and incomplete. Thankfully, the fulfillment that God offers is all encompassing and everlasting.

God's Word is clear: fulfillment through Christ is available to all who seek it and claim it. Count yourself among that number. Seek first a personal, transforming relationship with Jesus, and then claim the joy, the fulfillment, and the spiritual abundance that the Shepherd offers His sheep.

❪ *Find satisfaction in him who made you, and only then find satisfaction in yourself as part of his creation.*

St. Augustine

❪ *In serving we uncover the greatest fulfillment within and become a stellar example of a woman who knows and loves Jesus.*

Vonette Bright

A Helping Hand

But he who is greatest among you shall be your servant.
And whoever exalts himself will be humbled,
and he who humbles himself will be exalted.

Matthew 23:11-12 NKJV

⊰ If ever there was an example of generosity, it is Jesus. He lived generously, serving mankind, and He taught generosity.

He taught us that the most esteemed men and women are not the self-congratulatory leaders of society but are, instead, the humblest of servants. If you were being graded on generosity, how would you score? Would you earn "A"s in philanthropy and humility? Hopefully so. But if your grades could stand a little improvement, this is the perfect day to begin.

Today, you may feel the urge to hoard your blessings. Don't do it. Instead, give generously to your neighbors, and do so without fanfare. Find a need and fill it…humbly. Lend a helping hand and share a word of kindness…anonymously. This is God's way.

⊰ *The happiest and most joyful people are those who give money and serve.*

Dave Ramsey

⊰ *A cheerful giver does not count the cost of what he gives. His heart is set on pleasing and cheering him to whom the gift is given.*

Juliana of Norwich

TRUST HIM TO GUIDE YOU

*Trust the Lord with all your heart, and don't depend on
your own understanding. Remember the Lord
in all you do, and he will give you success.*

Proverbs 3:5-6 NCV

❧ Christ has already fought and won our battle for
us—He did so on the cross at Calvary. But despite
Christ's sacrifice, and despite God's promises, we
may become confused or disoriented by the endless
complications and countless distractions.

If you're unsure of your next step, lean upon God's
promises and lift your prayers to Him. Remember that
God is your protector. Open yourself to His heart, and
trust Him to guide you. When you do, God will direct
your steps, and you will receive His blessings today,
tomorrow, and throughout eternity.

❧ *It is a joy that God never abandons His children. He
guides faithfully all who listen to His directions.*

Corrie ten Boom

❧ *God will prove to you how good and acceptable and
perfect His will is when He's got His hands on the steering
wheel of your life.*

Stuart & Jill Briscoe

EXPECTING THE BEST

*May the Lord bless you and keep you. May the Lord
show you his kindness and have mercy on you.*

Numbers 6:24-25 NCV

❧ The familiar words of Psalm 118:24 remind us of a
profound yet simple truth: "This is the day which the
LORD hath made; we will rejoice and be glad in it"
(KJV). What do you expect from the day ahead? Are
you expecting God to do wonderful things, or are you
living beneath a cloud of apprehension and doubt?

For Christian believers, every day begins and
ends with God's Son and God's promises. When we
accept Christ into our hearts, God promises us the
opportunity for earthy peace and spiritual abundance.
But more importantly, God promises us the priceless
gift of eternal life.

As we face the inevitable challenges of life, we
must arm ourselves with the promises of God's Holy
Word. When we do, we can expect the best, not only
for the day ahead, but also for all eternity.

❧ *When I consider my existence beyond the grace, I am
filled with confidence and gratitude because God has made
an inviolable commitment to take me to heaven on the
merits of Christ.*

Bill Hybels

A ONE-OF-A-KIND TREASURE

Every word of God is pure;
He is a shield to those who put their trust in Him.

Proverbs 30:5 NKJV

❧ God's Word is a roadmap for our journey of life. As Christians, we are called upon to study God's Holy Word, to trust its promises, to follow its commandments, and to share its Good News with the world.

As believers, we must study the Bible and meditate upon its meaning for our lives. Otherwise, we deprive ourselves of a priceless gift from our Creator. God's Holy Word is, indeed, a transforming, life-changing, one-of-a-kind treasure. And, a passing acquaintance with the Good Book is insufficient for Christians who seek to obey God's Word and to understand His will. After all, neither man nor woman should live by bread alone.

❧ *The Gospel is not so much a demand as it is an offer, an offer of new life to man by the grace of God.*

E. Stanley Jones

❧ *If your Bible is falling apart, chances are your life is staying together.*

Anonymous

His Healing Touch

I am the Lord who heals you.

Exodus 15:26 NCV

God's Word has much to say about every aspect of your life, including your health. Are you concerned about your spiritual, physical, or emotional health? If so, there is a timeless source of comfort and assurance that is as near your bookshelf. That source is the Holy Bible.

And, when you face concerns of any sort—including health-related challenges—God is with You. So trust your medical doctor to do his or her part, but place your ultimate trust in your benevolent Heavenly Father. His healing touch, like His love, endures forever.

Jesus Christ is the One by Whom, for Whom, through Whom everything was made. Therefore, He knows what's wrong in your life and how to fix it.

Anne Graham Lotz

Sometimes we get tired of the burdens of life, but we know that Jesus Christ will meet us at the end of life's journey. And, that makes all the difference.

Billy Graham

A God-Made Man

Respecting the Lord and not being proud
will bring you wealth, honor, and life.

Proverbs 22:4 NCV

❧ We all owe countless debts that we can never repay. Our first debt, of course, is to our Father in heaven— Who has given us everything that we are and will ever be—and to His Son Who sacrificed His own life so that we might live eternally. We are also indebted to ancestors, parents, teachers, friends, spouses, family members, coworkers, fellow believers…and the list, of course, goes on.

Many of us, it seems, are more than willing to proclaim, "Look at all the wonderful things that I did!" But in our better moments, in the quiet moments when we search the depths of our own hearts, we know better. Whatever "it" is, God did that. And He deserves both the credit and the praise.

❧ *As children observe an attitude and spirit of humility in us, our example will pave the way for them when they must admit to their heavenly Father their own desperate need for guidance and forgiveness.*

Annie Chapman

❧ *Humility is a grace in the soul. It is indescribable wealth, a name and a gift from God.*

John Climacus

A GODLY LEADER

But a good leader plans to do good,
and those good things make him a good leader.

Isaiah 32:8 NCV

Warren Wiersbe counseled, "When God wants to accomplish something, He calls dedicated men and women to challenge His people and lead the way." Today more than ever, our world needs Christian leaders who willingly honor God with their words and their deeds, but not necessarily in that order.

If you seek to be a godly leader, then you must begin by being a worthy example to your family, to your friends, to your church, and to your community. After all, your words of instruction will never ring true unless you yourself are willing to follow them.

Are you the kind of leader whom you would want to follow? If so, congratulations. But if the answer to that question is no, then it's time to improve your leadership skills, beginning with the words that you speak and the example that you set, but not necessarily in that order.

If leadership equals influence, all Christian women have the opportunity to influence others. In the roles of wives, mothers, daughters, and friends, we influence through our words and our lives.

Susan Hunt

MENTORS THAT MATTER

Good people's words will help many others.

Proverbs 10:21 NCV

⮾ When you emulate godly people, you become a more godly person yourself. That's why you should seek out mentors who, by their words and their presence, make you a better person and a better Christian. Here's a simple yet effective way to strengthen your faith: Choose role models whose faith in God is strong.

Today, as a gift to yourself, select, from your friends and family members, a mentor whose judgement you trust. Then listen carefully to your mentor's advice and be willing to accept that advice, even if accepting it requires effort, or pain, or both. Consider your mentor to be God's gift to you. Thank God for that gift, and use it for the glory of His kingdom.

⮾ *Do not open your heart to every man, but discuss your affairs with one who is wise and who fears God.*

Thomas à Kempis

⮾ *It takes a wise person to give good advice, but an even wiser person to take it.*

Marie T. Freeman

THE GUIDEBOOK

All Scripture is given by inspiration of God,
and is profitable for doctrine, for reproof, for correction,
for instruction in righteousness, that the man of God
may be complete, thoroughly equipped
for every good work.

2 Timothy 3:16–17 NKJV

God has given us the Bible for the purpose of knowing His promises, His power, His commandments, His wisdom, His love, and His Son. As we study God's teachings and apply them to our lives, we live by the Word that shall never pass away. This guidebook for righteous living contains thorough instructions which, if followed, lead to fulfillment and salvation. But, if we choose to ignore God's commandments, the results are as predictable as they are tragic.

Today, let us follow God's commandments, and let us conduct our lives in such a way that we might be shining examples to our families, and, most importantly, to those who have not yet found Christ.

The Bible is a Christian's guidebook, and I believe the knowledge it sheds on pain and suffering is the great antidote to fear for suffering people. Knowledge can dissolve fear as light destroys darkness.

Philip Yancey

YOUR REAL RICHES

And he said: "Naked I came from my mother's womb,
And naked shall I return there.
The Lord gave, and the Lord has taken away;
Blessed be the name of the Lord."

Job 1:21 NKJV

❧ Charles Swindol was correct when he wrote, "When possessions become our god, we become materialistic and greedy . . . and we forfeit our contentment and our joy." It's a fact: material possessions can be much more trouble than they are worth.

Of course we live in a world in which a certain level of financial security is to be desired. But spiritual prosperity is profoundly more important than financial prosperity.

So the next time you're tempted to invest too much time and energy chasing material wealth, remember this: Your real riches are not of this world. You'll never really be rich until you are rich in spirit.

❧ *When we put people before possessions in our hearts, we are sowing seeds of enduring satisfaction.*

Beverly LaHaye

❧ *He is no fool who gives what he cannot keep to gain what he cannot lose.*

Jim Elliot

GOD WANTS TO USE YOU

To everything there is a season,
a time for every purpose under heaven.

Ecclesiastes 3:1 NKJV

⌘ God has things He wants you to do and places He wants you to go.

The most important decision of your life is your commitment to accept Jesus Christ as your personal Lord and Savior. And, once your eternal destiny is secured, you will undoubtedly ask yourself the question "What's next?" If you earnestly seek God's will for your life, you will find it…in time.

You may be certain that God is planning to use you in surprising, wonderful ways. And you may be certain that He intends to lead you along a path of His choosing. Your task is to watch for His signs, to listen to His words, to obey His commandments, and to follow where He leads.

⌘ *The place where God calls you is the place where your deep gladness and the world's deep hunger meet.*

Frederick Buechner

⌘ *The only Person who has ever brought sustained power and purpose into my life is the living person of God. The only words that keep making sense are His words. The only way that always stands is His way.*

Angela Thomas

THE SIMPLE LIFE

There is one who makes himself rich, yet has nothing;
And one who makes himself poor, yet has great riches.

Proverbs 13:7 NKJV

⇥ Think for a moment about the complexity of your life and compare it to the lives of your ancestors. Certainly, you are the beneficiary of many technological innovations, but those innovations have a price: in all likelihood, your world is highly complex. You live in a world where simplicity is in short supply.

Unless you take firm control of your time and your life, you may be overwhelmed by an ever-increasing tidal wave of complexity that threatens your happiness. But your Heavenly Father understands the joy of living simply, and so should you. So do yourself a favor: keep your life as simple as possible. Simplicity is, indeed, genius. By simplifying your life, you are destined to improve it.

⇥ *Prescription for a happier and healthier life: resolve to slow down your pace; learn to say no gracefully; resist the temptation to chase after more pleasure, more hobbies, and more social entanglements.*

James Dobson

⇥ *Nobody is going to simplify your life for you. You've got to simplify things for yourself.*

Marie T. Freeman

CHRIST'S LOVE CHANGES EVERYTHING.

Your old sinful self has died, and your new life
is kept with Christ in God.

Colossians 3:3 NCV

⍦ What does the love of Christ mean to His believers? In a world where hope is in short supply, the love of Christ means everything. And Christ's love changes everything. His love is perfect and steadfast. Even though we are fallible, and wayward, the Good Shepherd cares for us still. Even though we have fallen far short of the Father's commandments, Christ loves us with a power and depth that is beyond our understanding.

As we accept Christ's love and walk in Christ's footsteps, our lives bear testimony to His power and to His grace. Yes, Christ's love changes everything; may we invite Him into our hearts so it can then change everything in us.

⍦ *There is not a single thing that Jesus cannot change, control, and conquer because He is the living Lord.*

Franklin Graham

⍦ *I am Thine, O Lord; I have heard Thy voice, And it told Thy love to me. But I long to rise in the arms of faith And be closer drawn to Thee.*

Fanny Crosby

LOST IN THE CROWD

The fear of man brings a snare,
but whoever trusts in the Lord shall be safe.

Proverbs 29:25 NKJV

Whom will you try to please today: your God or your associates? Rick Warren observed, "Those who follow the crowd usually get lost in it." We know these words to be true, but oftentimes we fail to live by them.

Instead of trusting God for guidance, we imitate our neighbors and suffer the consequences. Instead of seeking to please our Father in heaven, we strive to please our peers, with decidedly mixed results.

Your obligation is most certainly not to neighbors, to friends, or even to family members. Your obligation is to an all-knowing, all-powerful God. You must seek to please Him first and always. No exceptions.

There is nothing that makes more cowards and feeble men that public opinion.

Henry Ward Beecher

It is comfortable to know that we are responsible to God and not to man. It is a small matter to be judged of man's judgement.

Lottie Moon

LIVING RIGHTEOUSLY

*Flee also youthful lusts; but pursue righteousness,
faith, love, peace with those who call on the Lord
out of a pure heart.*

2 Timothy 2:22 NKJV

A life of righteousness is lived in accordance with God's commandments. A thoughtful believer strives to be faithful, honest, generous, disciplined, loving, kind, humble, and grateful, to name only a few of the more obvious qualities which are described in God's Word.

If we seek to follow the steps of Jesus, we must seek to live according to His teachings. In short, we must, to the best of our abilities, live according to the principles contained in the Holy Bible. When we do, we become powerful examples to our families and friends of the abundant hope that God bestows upon the righteous.

We are in desperate need for people of faith who are willing to courageously stand against sin and stand for righteousness.

Susan Hunt

We must appropriate the tender mercy of God every day after conversion, or problems quickly develop. We need his grace daily in order to live a righteous life.

Jim Cymbala

STRENGTH FOR THE STRUGGLE

*My grace is sufficient for you, for My strength is
made perfect in weakness.*

2 Corinthians 12:9 NKJV

Has your faith been put to the test yet? If so, then
you know that with God's help, you can endure
life's darker days. And if you have not yet faced the
inevitable trials and tragedies of life, you will.

Life is a tapestry of good days and difficult days,
with good days predominating. During the good days,
we are tempted to take our blessings for granted (a
temptation that we must resist with all our might).
But, during life's difficult days, we discover precisely
what we're made of. And more importantly, we
discover what our faith is made of.

And when your faith is put to the test, rest assured
that God is perfectly willing—and always ready—to
give you strength for the struggle.

*I believe that the Creator of this universe takes delight in
turning the terrors and tragedies that come with living in
this old, fallen domain of the devil and transforming them
into something that strengthens our hope, tests our faith,
and shows forth His glory.*

Al Green

HOPE FOR AN ANXIOUS WORLD

Be humble under God's powerful hand so he will lift you up when the right time comes. Give all your worries to him, because he cares about you.

1 Peter 5:6-7 NCV

When calamity strikes anywhere in the world, we may be confronted with real-time images, images that breed anxiety. And as we stare transfixed at our television screens, we may fall prey to fear, discouragement, worry, or all three. But our Father in Heaven has other plans. God has promised that we may lead lives of abundance, not anxiety. In fact, His Word instructs us to "be anxious for nothing" (Philippians 4:6). But how can we put our fears to rest? By taking those fears to God and leaving them there.

As you face the challenges of daily life, you may find yourself becoming anxious. If so, turn every one of your concerns over to your Heavenly Father. The same God who created the universe will comfort you if you ask Him…so ask Him and trust Him. And then watch in amazement as your anxieties melt into the warmth of His loving hands.

One of the main missions of God is to free us from the debilitating bonds of fear and anxiety. God's heart is broken when He sees us so demoralized and weighed down by fear.

Bill Hybels

BEYOND BITTERNESS

If someone does wrong to you, do not pay him back
by doing wrong to him.
Try to do what everyone thinks is right.

Romans 12:17 NCV

❧ Bitterness is a spiritual sickness. It will consume your soul; it is dangerous to your emotional health. It can destroy you if you let it . . . so don't let it!

If you are caught up in intense feelings of anger or resentment, you know all too well the destructive power of these emotions. How can you rid yourself of these feelings? First, you must prayerfully ask God to cleanse your heart. Then, you must learn to catch yourself whenever thoughts of bitterness or hatred begin to attack you. Your challenge is this: You must learn to resist negative thoughts before they hijack your emotions.

Matthew 5:22 teaches us that if we judge others, we, too, will be subject to judgement. Let us refrain, then, from judging our neighbors. Instead, let us forgive them and love them, while leaving their judgement to a far more capable authority: the One who sits on His throne in heaven.

❧ *Bitterness is a spiritual cancer, a rapidly growing malignancy that can consume your life. Bitterness cannot be ignored but must be healed at the very core, and only Christ can heal bitterness.*

Beth Moore

BORN AGAIN

You have been born again, and this new life did not come
from something that dies, but from something that cannot
die. You were born again through God's living message
that continues forever.

1 Peter 1:23 NCV

❧ Christ sacrificed His life so that we might be born again. This gift, freely given from God's only begotten Son, is the priceless possession of everyone who accepts Him as Lord and Savior.

Let us claim Christ's gift today. Let us walk with the Savior, let us love Him, let us praise Him, and let us share His message of salvation with all those who cross our paths.

The comforting words of Ephesians 2:8 make God's promise clear: "For by grace you have been saved through faith, and that not of yourselves; it is the gift of God" (NKJV). Thus, we are saved not because of our good deeds but because of our faith in Christ. May we, who have been given so much, praise our Savior for the gift of salvation, and may we share the joyous news of our Master's limitless love with our families, with our friends, and with the world.

❧ *Being born again is God's solution to our need for love and life and light.*

Anne Graham Lotz

MID-COURSE CORRECTIONS

The wise see danger ahead and avoid it,
but fools keep going and get into trouble.

Proverbs 27:12 NCV

❧ Are you facing one of life's inevitable "mid-course corrections"? If so, you must place your faith, your trust, and your life in the hands of the One who does not change: your Heavenly Father.

In our fast-paced world, everyday life has become an exercise in managing change. Our circumstances change; our relationships change; our bodies change. We grow older every day, as does our world. Thankfully, God does not change. He is eternal, as are the truths that are found in His Holy Word.

He is the unmoving rock upon which you must construct this day and every day. When you do, you are secure.

❧ *We do not love each other without changing each other. We do not observe the world around us without in some way changing it, and being changed ourselves.*

Madeleine L'Engle

❧ *Sometimes your medicine bottle says, "Shake well before using." That is what God has to do with some of his people. He has to shake them well before they are usable.*

Vance Havner

A RELATIONSHIP THAT HONORS GOD

I am always praising you; all day long I honor you.

Psalm 71:8 NCV

As you think about the nature of your relationship with God, remember this: you will always have some type of relationship with Him—it is inevitable that your life must be lived in relationship to God. The question is not if you will have a relationship with Him; the burning question is whether or not that relationship will be one that seeks to honor Him . . . or not.

Are you willing to place God first in your life? And, are you willing to welcome God's Son into your heart? Unless you can honestly answer these questions with a resounding yes, then your relationship with God isn't what it could be or should be. Thankfully, God is always available, He's always ready to forgive, and He's waiting to hear from you now. The rest, of course, is up to you.

The Holy Spirit testifies of Jesus. So when you are filled with the Holy Spirit, you speak about our Lord and really live to His honor.

Corrie ten Boom

Our progress in holiness depends on God and ourselves—on God's grace and on our will to be holy.

Mother Teresa

COMFORTING OTHERS

Bear one another's burdens,
and so fulfill the law of Christ.

Galatians 6:2 NKJV

❧ We live in a world that is, on occasion, a frightening place. Sometimes, we sustain life-altering losses that are so profound and so tragic that it seems we could never recover. But, with God's help and with the help of encouraging family members and friends, we can recover.

In times of need, God's Word is clear: as believers, we must offer comfort to those in need by sharing not only our courage but also our faith. As the renowned revivalist Vance Havner observed, "No journey is complete that does not lead through some dark valleys. We can properly comfort others only with the comfort wherewith we ourselves have been comforted of God." Enough said.

❧ *So often we think that to be encouragers we have to produce great words of wisdom when, in fact, a few simple syllables of sympathy and an arm around the shoulder can often provide much needed comfort.*

Florence Littauer

BEYOND THE DIFFICULTIES

*It will be hard when all these things happen to you.
But after that you will come back to the Lord your God
and obey him, because the Lord your God is a merciful
God. He will not leave you or destroy you.
He will not forget the Agreement with your ancestors,
which he swore to them.*

Deuteronomy 4:30-31 NCV

❧ Sometimes the traffic jams, and sometimes the dog gobbles the homework. But, when we find ourselves overtaken by the minor frustrations of life, we must catch ourselves, take a deep breath, and lift our thoughts upward. Although we are here on earth struggling to rise above the distractions of the day, we need never struggle alone. God is here—eternally and faithfully, with infinite patience and love—and, if we reach out to Him, He will restore perspective and peace to our souls.

If you find yourself enduring difficult circumstances, remember that God remains in His heaven. If you become discouraged with the direction of your day or your life, lift your thoughts and prayers to Him. He will guide you through your difficulties and beyond them.

❧ *Whatever hallway you're in—no matter how long, how dark, or how scary—God is right there with you.*

Bill Hybels

LET GOD DECIDE

A man's heart plans his way,
but the Lord directs his steps.

Proverbs 16:9 NKJV

❧ The world will often lead you astray, but God will not. His counsel leads you to Himself, which, of course, is the path He has always intended for you to take. Are you facing a difficult decision, a troubling circumstance, or a powerful temptation? If so, it's time to step back, to stop focusing on the world, and to focus, instead, on the will of your Father in heaven.

Everyday living is an exercise in decision-making. Today and every day you must make choices: choices about what you will do, what you will worship, and how you will think. When in doubt, make choices that you sincerely believe will bring you to a closer relationship with God. And if you're uncertain of your next step, pray about it. When you do, answers will come—the right answers for you.

❧ God *always gives His best to those who leave the choice with Him.*

Jim Elliot

❧ *When we learn to listen to Christ's voice for the details of our daily decisions, we begin to know Him personally.*

Catherine Marshall

WRESTLING WITH OUR DOUBTS

*Immediately the father of the child cried out and said
with tears, "Lord, I believe; help my unbelief!"*

Mark 9:24 NKJV

❧ Even the most faithful Christians are overcome by
occasional bouts of uncertainty and doubt. You are no
exception. You are a fallible human being, and just
because you are a follower of Christ doesn't mean you
will never experience times of doubt or fear.

When you feel that your faith is being tested to
its limits, seek the comfort and assurance of the One
who sent His Son as a sacrifice for you.

Even if you feel very distant from God, God is
never distant from you. When you sincerely seek His
presence, He will touch your heart, calm your fears,
and restore your faith in the future . . . and your faith
in Him.

❧ *We basically have two choices to make in dealing with
the mysteries of God. We can wrestle with Him or we can
rest in Him.*

Calvin Miller

❧ *To wrestle with God does not mean that we have lost
faith, but that we are fighting for it.*

Sheila Walsh

ENTHUSIASM FOR CHRIST

Rest your hope fully upon the grace that is to be brought to you at the revelation of Jesus Christ; as obedient children, not conforming yourselves to the former lusts, as in your ignorance; but as He who called you is holy, you also be holy in all your conduct.

1 Peter 1:13-15 NKJV

❧ When we fan the flames of enthusiasm for Christ, our faith serves as a beacon to others. John Wesley advised, "Catch on fire with enthusiasm and people will come for miles to watch you burn." His words still ring true.

Our world desperately needs faithful believers who share the Good News of Jesus with joyful exuberance. Be such a believer. The world desperately needs your enthusiasm—now!

❧ *We act as though comfort and luxury were the chief requirements of life, when all we need to make us really happy is something to be enthusiastic about.*

Charles Kingsley

❧ *Consider every day a new beginning, and always act with the same fervour as on the first day you began.*

Anthony of Padua

EXCUSES AND MORE EXCUSES

*Let us live in a right way . . . clothe yourselves with
the Lord Jesus Christ and forget about satisfying
your sinful self.*

Romans 13:13-14 NCV

❧ All too often we are quick to proclaim ourselves
"victims," and we refuse to take responsibility for
our actions. So we make excuses, excuses, and more
excuses—with predictably poor results.

We live in a world where excuses are everywhere.
When we hear the words, "I'm sorry but...", most of
us know exactly what is to follow: the excuse. The
dog ate the homework. Traffic was terrible. It's the
company's fault. The boss is to blame. The equipment
is broken. We're out of that. And so forth, and so on.

Because we humans are such creative excuse-
makers, all of the really good excuses have already
been taken. In fact, the high-quality excuses have
been used, re-used, over-used, and abused. That's why
excuses don't work—we've heard them all before.

So, if you're wasting your time trying to portray
yourself as a victim, or if you're trying to concoct
a new and improved excuse, don't bother. Excuses
don't work, and while you're inventing them, neither
do you.

❧ *Making up a string of excuses is usually harder than
doing the work.*

Marie T. Freeman

CALMING YOUR FEARS

Be not afraid; only believe.

Mark 5:36 NKJV

❧ We worry about the future and the past; we worry about finances and relationships. As we survey the landscape of our lives, we observe all manner of molehills and imagine them to be mountains. The irony is that most of the things we worry about will never come to pass, yet we worry still.

Are you concerned about the inevitable challenges that make up the fabric of everyday life? If so, why not ask God to help you regain a clear perspective about the problems (and opportunities) that confront you? When you petition your Heavenly Father sincerely and seek His guidance, He can touch your heart, clear your vision, renew your mind, and calm your fears.

❧ *God alone can give us songs in the night.*

C. H. Spurgeon

❧ *I have found the perfect antidote for fear. Whenever it sticks up its ugly face, I clobber it with prayer.*

Dale Evans Rogers

In His Hands

For whatever is born of God overcomes the world.
And this is the victory that has overcome
the world—our faith.

1 John 5:4 NKJV

❧ The first element of a successful life is faith: faith in God, faith in His Son, and faith in His promises. If we place our lives in God's hands, our faith is rewarded in ways that we—as human beings with clouded vision and limited understanding—can scarcely comprehend. But, if we seek to rely solely upon our own resources, or if we seek earthly success outside the boundaries of God's commandments, we reap a bitter harvest for ourselves and for our loved ones.

Do you desire the abundance and success that God has promised? Then trust Him today and every day that you live. Then, when you have entrusted your future to the Giver of all things good, rest assured that your future is secure, not only for today, but also for all eternity.

❧ *The Christian life is one of faith, where we find ourselves routinely overdriving our headlights but knowing it's okay because God is in control and has a purpose behind it.*

Bill Hybels

THE JOYS OF FRIENDSHIP

I thank my God upon every remembrance of you.

Philippians 1:3 NKJV

❧ What is a friend? The dictionary defines the word friend as "a person who is attached to another by feelings of affection or personal regard." This definition is accurate, as far as it goes, but when we examine the deeper meaning of friendship, so many more descriptors come to mind: trustworthiness, loyalty, helpfulness, kindness, encouragement, humor, and cheerfulness, to mention but a few.

Today, as you consider the many blessings that God has given you, remember to thank Him for the friends He has chosen to place along your path. May you be a blessing to them, and may they richly bless you today, tomorrow, and every day that you live.

❧ *No medicine is more valuable, none more efficacious, none better suited to the cure of all our temporal ills than a friend to whom we may turn for consolation in time of trouble.*

St. Aelred

❧ *Nothing opens the heart like a true friend, to whom you may impart griefs, joys, fears, fears, hopes, suspicions, counsels, and whatever lies upon the heart.*

Francis Bacon

THE SHEPHERD'S CARE

God, your justice reaches to the skies.
You have done great things;
God, there is no one like you.

Psalms 71:19 NCV

❧ It's a promise that is made over and over again in the Bible: Whatever "it" is, God can handle it. When we're worried, God can reassure us; when we're sad, God can comfort us. When our hearts are broken, God is not just near, He is here. So we must lift our thoughts and prayers to Him. When we do, He will answer our prayers. Why? Because He is our shepherd, and He has promised to protect us now and forever.

Are you facing challenges that leave you fearful or discouraged? If so, you need not carry your burdens alone. God is ready to help . . . and the next move is yours.

❧ *Cast your cares on God; that anchor holds.*

Alfred, Lord Tennyson

❧ *When considering the size of your problems, there are two categories that you should never worry about: the problems that are small enough for you to handle, and the ones that aren't too big for God to handle.*

Marie T. Freeman

GOD'S LOVE

He who does not love does not know God,
for God is love.

1 John 4:8 NKJV

❧ God loves you. He loves you more than you can imagine; His affection is deeper than you can fathom. God made you in His own image and gave you salvation through the person of His Son Jesus Christ. And as a result, you have an important decision to make. You must decide what to do about God's love: you can return it . . . or not.

When you accept the love that flows from the heart of God, you are transformed. When you embrace God's love, you feel differently about yourself, your neighbors, your community, your church, and your world. When you open your heart to God's love, you will feel compelled to share God's message—and His compassion—with others. God's heart is overflowing—accept His love; return His love; and share His love. Today.

❧ *Our hearts have been made to cry out for a love that can come only from our Creator.*

Angela Thomas

❧ *O the deep, deep love of Jesus, vast, unmeasured, boundless, and free; rolling as a mighty ocean in its fullness over me.*

Samuel Trevor Francis

BLESSED BEYOND MEASURE

The Lord bless you and keep you;
The Lord make His face shine upon you,
And be gracious to you.

Numbers 6:24-25 NKJV

❧ Psalm 145 makes this promise: "The LORD is gracious and full of compassion, slow to anger and great in mercy. The LORD is good to all, and His tender mercies are over all His works" (8-9 NKJV). As God's children, we are blessed beyond measure, but sometimes, as busy citizens of a fast-paced world, we are slow to give thanks to the Giver.

The gifts we receive from God are multiplied when we share them with others. May we always give thanks to God for our blessings, and may we always demonstrate our gratitude by sharing them.

❧ Let's never forget that some of God's greatest mercies are His refusals. He says no in order that He may, in some way we cannot imagine, say yes. All His ways with us are merciful. His meaning is always love.

Elisabeth Elliot

❧ God's love for His children in unconditional, no strings attached. But, God's blessings on our lives do come with a condition—obedience.

Jim Gallery

A SIMPLE GOLDEN RULE

Do to others what you want them to do to you.

Matthew 7:12 NCV

❧ Would you like to make the world a better place? If so, you can start by practicing the Golden Rule.

Is the Golden Rule your rule, or is it just another Bible verse that goes in one ear and out the other? Jesus made Himself perfectly clear: He instructed you to treat other people in the same way that you want to be treated. But sometimes, especially when you're feeling pressures or everyday living, obeying the Golden Rule can seem like an impossible task—but it's not. So if you want to know how to treat other people, ask the person you see every time you look into the mirror. The answer you receive will tell you exactly what to do.

❧ *It is one of the most beautiful compensations of life that no one can sincerely try to help another without helping herself.*

Barbara Johnson

❧ *It is wrong for anyone to be anxious to receive more from his neighbor than he himself is willing to give to God.*

St. Francis of Assisi

OPPORTUNITIES: THEY'RE EVERYWHERE

Be wise in the way you act with people who are not
believers, making the most of every opportunity.

Colossians 4:5 NCV

❧ Whether you realize it or not, opportunities are whirling around you like stars crossing the night sky: beautiful to observe but too numerous to count. Yet you may be too wrapped up in the daily grind to notice.

Take time to step back from the challenges of everyday living so that you can focus your thoughts on two things: the talents God has given you and the opportunities that He has placed before you. God is leading you in the direction of those opportunities. Your task is to watch carefully, to pray fervently, and to act accordingly.

❧ *Those who are fired with an enthusiastic idea and who allow it to take hold and dominate their thoughts find that new worlds open for them. As long as enthusiasm holds out, so will new opportunities.*

Norman Vincent Peale

❧ *Every day we live is a priceless gift of God, loaded with possibilities to learn something new, to gain fresh insights.*

Dale Evans Rogers

LOOK BEFORE YOU LEAP

Patience is better than strength.

Proverbs 16:32 NCV

❧ Are you, at times, just a little bit impulsive? Do you sometimes forget to look before you leap? If so, God wants to have a little chat with you.

God's Word is clear: as believers, we are called to lead lives of discipline, diligence, moderation, and maturity. But the world often tempts us to behave otherwise. Everywhere we turn, or so it seems, we are faced with powerful temptations to behave in undisciplined, ungodly ways.

God's Word instructs us to be disciplined in our thoughts and our actions; God's Word warns us against the dangers of impulsive behavior. As believers in a just God, we should act and react accordingly.

❧ *We will always experience regret when we live for the moment and do not weigh our words and deeds before we give them life.*

Lisa Bevere

❧ *Zeal without knowledge is always less useful and effective than regulated zeal, and very often is highly dangerous.*

St. Bernard of Clairvaux

A Shining Light

"While you have the light, believe in the light,
that you may become sons of light." These things
Jesus spoke, and departed, and was hidden from them.

John 12:36 NKJV

❧ The Bible clearly states that you are "the light that gives light to the world." What kind of light have you been giving off lately? Hopefully, you've been a good example for all to see. Why? Because the world needs all the light it can get, and that includes your light, too.

Christ showed enduring love for you by willingly sacrificing His own life so that you might have eternal life. As a response to His sacrifice, you should love Him, praise Him, and share His message of salvation with your neighbors and with the world. So let your light shine today and every day. When you do, God will bless you now and forever.

❧ *You can't light another's path without casting light on your own.*

John Maxwell

❧ *Light is stronger than darkness—darkness cannot "comprehend" or "overcome" it.*

Anne Graham Lotz

THE LESSONS OF TOUGH TIMES

I waited patiently for the LORD;
And He inclined to me, And heard my cry.

Psalm 40:1 NKJV

❧ Have you experienced a recent setback? If so, look for the lesson that God is trying to teach you. Instead of complaining about life's sad state of affairs, learn what needs to be learned, change what needs to be changed, and move on. View failure as an opportunity to reassess God's will for your life. And while you're at it, consider life's inevitable disappointments to be powerful opportunities to learn more—more about yourself, more about your circumstances, and more about your world.

Life can be difficult at times. And everybody (including you) makes mistakes. Your job is to make them only once. And how can you do that? By learning the lessons of tough times sooner rather than later, that's how.

❧ *God is able to take mistakes, when they are committed to Him, and make of them something for our good and for His glory.*

Ruth Bell Graham

❧ *Father, take our mistakes and turn them into opportunities.*

Max Lucado

GIVE ME PATIENCE, LORD, RIGHT NOW!

Now we exhort you, brethren, warn those who are unruly, comfort the fainthearted, uphold the weak, be patient with all.

1 Thessalonians 5:14 NKJV

❧ Most of us are impatient for God to grant us the desires of our heart. Usually, we know what we want, and we know precisely when we want it: right now, if not sooner. But God may have other plans. And when God's plans differ from our own, we must trust in His infinite wisdom and in His infinite love.

As busy men and women living in a fast-paced world, many of us find that waiting quietly for God is difficult. Why? Because we are fallible human beings seeking to live according to our own timetables, not God's. In our better moments, we realize that patience is not only a virtue, it is also a commandment from God.

God instructs us to be patient in all things. We must be patient with our families, our friends, and our associates. We must also be patient with our Creator as He unfolds His plan for our lives. And that's as it should be. After all, think how patient God has been with us.

❧ *Our challenge is to wait in faith for the day of God's favor and salvation.*

Jim Cymbala

KEEP POSSESSIONS IN PERSPECTIVE

And He said to them, "Take heed and beware of
covetousness, for one's life does not consist in
the abundance of the things he possesses."

Luke 12:15 NKJV

❧ Our material possessions have the potential to do great good or terrible harm, depending upon how we choose to use them. All too often, we focus our thoughts and energies on the accumulation of earthly treasures, leaving precious little time to accumulate the only treasures that really matter: the spiritual kind. As believers, our instructions are clear: we must use our possessions in accordance with God's commandments, and we must be faithful stewards of the gifts He has seen fit to bestow upon us.

Today, let us honor God by placing no other gods before Him. God comes first; everything else comes next—and "everything else" most certainly includes all of our earthly possessions.

❧ *I have held many things in my hands, and I have lost them all; but whatever I have placed in God's hands, that I still possess.*

Corrie ten Boom

❧ *Nobody can fight properly and boldly for the faith if he clings to a fear of being stripped of earthly possessions.*

St. Peter Damian

COMMUNITY LIFE

We do not need to write you about having love for
your Christian family, because God has already
taught you to love each other.

1 Thessalonians 4:9 NCV

As we travel along life's road, we build lifelong relationships with a small, dear circle of family and friends. And how best do we build and maintain these relationships? By following the Word of God.

Healthy relationships are built upon honesty, compassion, responsible behavior, trust, and optimism. Healthy relationships are built upon the Golden Rule. Healthy relationships are built upon sharing and caring. All of these principles are found time and time again in God's Holy Word. When we read God's Word and follow His commandments, we enrich our own lives and the lives of those who are closest to us.

Horizontal relationships—relationships between people—are crippled at the outset unless the vertical relationship—the relationship between each person and God—is in place.

Ed Young

Line by line, moment by moment, special times are etched into our memories in the permanent ink of everlasting love in our relationships.

Gloria Gaither

GOOD THINKING

Be careful what you think,
because your thoughts run your life.

Proverbs 4:23 NCV

❧ When you decided to allow Christ to rule over your heart, you entitled yourself to share in His promise of spiritual abundance and eternal joy. Have you claimed that entitlement? Are you an upbeat believer? Are you a person whose hopes and dreams are alive and well? Hopefully so. But sometimes, when pessimism and doubt invade your thoughts, you won't feel like celebrating. Why? Because thoughts are intensely powerful things.

You may need to spend more time thinking about your blessings, and less time fretting about your hardships. Then, take time to thank the Giver of all things good for gifts that are, in truth, far too numerous to count.

❧ *As we have by faith said no to sin, so we should by faith say yes to God and set our minds on things above, where Christ is seated in the heavenlies.*

Vonette Bright

❧ *Your thoughts are the determining factor as to whose mold you are conformed to. Control your thoughts and you control the direction of your life.*

Charles Stanley

ANSWERING OUR DOUBTS

*For we do not want you to be ignorant, brethren,
of our trouble which came to us in Asia: that we were
burdened beyond measure, above strength, so that we
despaired even of life. Yes, we had the sentence of death
in ourselves, that we should not trust in ourselves but in
God who raises the dead, who delivered us from so great
a death, and does deliver us; in whom we trust
that He will still deliver us.*

2 Corinthians 1:8-10 NKJV

❧ When worries and doubts go unchecked, despair is soon to follow. Doubts come in several shapes and sizes: doubts about God, doubts about the future, and doubts about our own abilities, for starters. But when doubts creep in, as they will from time to time, we need not despair. As Sheila Walsh observed, "To wrestle with God does not mean that we have lost faith, but that we are fighting for it."

God never leaves our side, not for an instant. He is always with us, always willing to calm the storms of life. When we sincerely seek His presence—and when we genuinely seek to establish a deeper, more meaningful relationship Him—God is prepared to touch our hearts, to calm our fears, to answer our doubts, and to restore our confidence.

❧ *It is certainly wrong to despair. And if despair is wrong, hope is right.*

John Lubbock

THANKSLIVING

In all your ways acknowledge Him,
and He shall direct your paths.

Proverbs 3:6 NKJV

❧ As believers who have been saved by a risen Christ, we are blessed beyond human comprehension. We who have been given so much should make thanksgiving a habit, a regular part of our daily routines.

Sometimes, daily life can be complicated and frustrating. When the demands of life leave us rushing from here to there with scarcely a moment to spare, we may not pause to thank our Creator for the countless blessings He bestows upon us—and we pay a price for our oversight.

Whenever we neglect to give proper thanks to the Giver of all things good, we suffer because of our misplaced priorities. Of course, God's gifts are too numerous to count, but we should attempt to count them nonetheless. We owe our Heavenly Father everything, including our eternal praise . . . starting this very moment.

❧ *The devil moves in when a Christian starts to complain, but thanksgiving in the Spirit defeats the devil and glorifies the Lord.*

Warren Wiersbe

FOLLOWING THE CROWD?

*He said to them, "You make yourselves look good
in front of people, but God knows what is really
in your hearts. What is important to people
is hateful in God's sight.*

Luke 16:15 NCV

❧ It's tempting to be more concerned with pleasing
people than with pleasing God . . . tempting but
wrong.

Whom will you try to please today: God or "the
crowd"? If you choose to follow the crowd, you may
find yourself headed directly for trouble, but If you
follow God and His only begotten Son, you'll be
safe.

Your obligation is most certainly not to neighbors,
to friends, to business associates, or even to family
members. Your obligation is to an all-knowing, all-
powerful God. You must seek to please Him first and
always. No exceptions.

❧ *Fashion is an enduring testimony to the fact that we
live quite consciously before the eyes of others.*

John Eldredge

❧ *It is comfortable to know that we are responsible to
God and not to man. It is a small matter to be judged of
man's judgement.*

Lottie Moon

ONE MOUTH, TWO EARS

*My dear brothers and sisters, always be willing to listen
and slow to speak. Do not become angry easily,
because anger will not help you live
the right kind of life God wants.*

James 1:19-20 NCV

❧ Anger is a natural human emotion that is sometimes necessary and appropriate. Even Jesus Himself became angered when He confronted the moneychangers in the temple. But, more often than not, our frustrations are of the more mundane variety.

Perhaps God gave each of us one mouth and two ears in order that we might listen twice as much as we speak. Unfortunately, many of us do otherwise, especially when we become angry.

When you are tempted to lose your temper over the minor inconveniences of life, don't. Turn away from anger, and turn instead to God.

❧ *Life is too short to spend it being angry, bored, or dull.*

Barbara Johnson

❧ *Fill the heart with the love of Christ so that only truth and purity can come out of the mouth.*

Warren Wiersbe

THANKSGIVING YES . . . ENVY NO!

Don't get angry. Don't be upset; it only leads to trouble.
Psalms 37:8 NCV

❧ You have every reason to celebrate life. God has promised you the opportunity to receive His abundance and His joy—in fact, you have the opportunity to receive those gifts right now. But if you allow envy to gnaw away at the fabric of your soul, you'll find that joy remains elusive. So do yourself an enormous favor: Rather than succumbing to the sin of envy, focus on the marvelous things that God has done for you—starting with Christ's sacrifice. Thank the Giver of all good gifts, and keep thanking Him for the wonders of His love and the miracles of His creation. Count your own blessings and let your neighbors count theirs. It's the godly way to live.

❧ *Contentment comes when we develop an attitude of gratitude for the important things we do have in our lives that we tend to take for granted if we have our eyes staring longingly at our neighbor's stuff.*

Dave Ramsey

❧ *Discontent dries up the soul.*

Elisabeth Elliot

NEW BEGINNINGS

Do not remember the former things, nor consider the things of old. Behold, I will do a new thing.

Isaiah 43:18-19 NKJV

❧ Each new day offers countless opportunities to serve God, to seek His will, and to obey His teachings. But each day also offers countless opportunities to stray from God's commandments and to wander far from His path.

Sometimes, we wander aimlessly in a wilderness of our own making, but God has better plans of us. And, whenever we ask Him to renew our strength and guide our steps, He does so.

Consider this day a new beginning. Consider it a fresh start, a renewed opportunity to serve your Creator with willing hands and a loving heart. Ask God to renew your sense of purpose as He guides your steps. Today is a glorious opportunity to serve your Father in heaven. Seize that opportunity while you can because tomorrow might be too late.

❧ *If the leaves had not been let go to fall and wither, if the tree had not consented to be a skeleton for many months, there would be no new life rising, no bud, no flower, no fruit, no seed, no new generation.*

Elisabeth Elliot

BEING PATIENT WITH OURSELVES

*Because you have these blessings, do your best to add
these things to your lives: to your faith, add goodness;
and to your goodness, add knowledge;
and to your knowledge, add self-control;
and to your self-control, add patience.*

2 Peter 1:5-6 NCV

❧ Being patient with other people can be difficult.
But sometimes, we find it even more difficult to be
patient with ourselves. We have high expectations
and lofty goals. We want to accomplish things now,
not later. And, of course, we want our lives to unfold
according to our own timetables, not God's.

Throughout the Bible, we are instructed that
patience is the companion of wisdom. God's message,
then, is clear: we must be patient with all people,
beginning with that particular person who stares back
at us each time we gaze into the mirror.

So if you happen to be your own worst critic—or if
you expect perfection from yourself (not to mention
others), it's time to reconsider. You don't have to be
perfect to be a spectacularly wonderful human being.

❧ *Let me encourage you to continue to wait with faith.
God may not perform a miracle, but He is trustworthy to
touch you and make you whole where there used to be a
hole.*

Lisa Welchel

CHOICES, CHOICES, CHOICES

*Our only goal is to please God whether we live
here or there, because we must all stand before
Christ to be judged.*

2 Corinthians 5:9-10 NCV

❧ Every life, including yours, is a tapestry of choices.
And the quality of your life depends, to a surprising
extent, on the quality of the choices you make.

Would you like to enjoy a life of abundance and
significance? If so, you must you must make choices
that are pleasing to God.

From the instant you wake up in the morning until
the moment you nod off to sleep at night, you make
lots of decisions: decisions about the things you do,
decisions about the words you speak, and decisions
about the thoughts you choose to think.

Today and every day, it's up to you (and only you)
to make wise choices, choices that enhance your
relationship with God. After all, He deserves no less
than your best . . . and so do you.

❧ *I believe with all my heart and soul that at every
important crossroads in my life I was faced with a choice:
between right and wrong, between serving God and
pleasing myself. I didn't always make the right choice.
But God heard the earnest prayers of those who loved me
and by His grace brought me to my knees.*

Al Green

GOD IS HERE

Come near to God, and God will come near to you.

James 4:8 NCV

❧ As you think about the day ahead, here's an important question to ask yourself: do you expect God to walk with you every step of the way? The answer to that question, of course, has nothing to do with God and everything to do with you. God will most certainly be there for you . . . will you be there with Him?

When you begin the day with prayer and praise, God often seems very near indeed. But, if you ignore God's presence or—worse yet—rebel against it altogether, the world in which you live becomes a spiritual wasteland.

The comforting words of Psalm 46:10 remind us to "Be still, and know that I am God." When we do so, we sense the loving presence of our Heavenly Father, and we are comforted by the certain knowledge that God is not far away . . . and He isn't even nearby. He is, quite literally, here. And it's up to each of us to sense His presence.

❧ *The things God delights in, kindness, justice, and righteousness, are the essence of Christianity. If he delights in these things, then his followers must also.*

Mary Morrison Suggs

WORDS OF HOPE

Wise people's minds tell them what to say,
and that helps them be better teachers.

Proverbs 16:23 NCV

☯ God's Word reminds us that "Careless words stab like a sword, but wise words bring healing" (Proverbs 12:18 NCV). If you seek to be a source of encouragement to friends, to family members and to coworkers, then you must measure your words carefully. And that's exactly what God wants you to do.

Today, make this promise to yourself: vow to be an honest, effective, encouraging communicator at work, at home, and everyplace in between. Speak wisely, not impulsively. Use words of kindness and praise, not words of anger or derision. Learn how to be truthful without being cruel. Remember that you have the power to heal others or to injure them, to lift others up or to hold them back. And when you learn how to lift them up, you'll soon discover that you've lifted yourself up, too.

☯ *Attitude and the spirit in which we communicate are as important as the words we say.*

Charles Stanley

☯ *Keeping the lines of communication open can help exterminate the pests that gnaw away at love.*

Annie Chapman

THE POWER OF FAITH

Have faith in the Lord your God, and you will stand strong. Have faith in his prophets, and you will succeed.

2 Chronicles 20:20 NCV

„ Every life—including yours—is a series of successes and failures, celebrations and disappointments, joys and sorrows. Every step of the way, through every triumph and tragedy, God will stand by your side and strengthen you . . . if you have faith in Him. Jesus taught His disciples that if they had faith, they could move mountains. You can too.

When you place your faith, your trust, indeed your life in the hands of Christ Jesus, you'll be amazed at the marvelous things He can do with you and through you. So strengthen your faith through praise, through worship, through Bible study, and through prayer. And trust God's plans. With Him, all things are possible, and He stands ready to open a world of possibilities to you . . . if you have faith.

„ *O holy Savior, Friend unseen, The faint, the weak on Thee may lean, Help me, throughout life's varying scene, By faith to cling to Thee.*

Charlotte Elliott

„ *Let your faith in Christ be in the quiet confidence that He will, every day and every moment, give you the strength you need.*

Andrew Murray

SOLVING THE RIDDLES

*But if any of you needs wisdom, you should ask God
for it. He is generous and enjoys giving to all people,
so he will give you wisdom.*

James 1:5 NCV

❧ Are you facing a difficult decision? Take your
concerns to God and avail yourself of the messages
and mentors that He has placed along your path.
Life presents each of us with countless questions,
conundrums, doubts, and problems. Thankfully, the
riddles of everyday living are not too difficult to solve
if we look for answers in the right places. When we
have questions, we should consult God's Word, we
should seek the guidance of the Holy Spirit, and we
should trust the counsel of God-fearing friends and
family members.

When you do, God will speak to you in His own
way and in His own time, and when He does, you can
most certainly trust the answers that He gives.

❧ *As we trust God to give us wisdom for today's
decisions, He will lead us a step at a time into what He
wants us to be doing in the future.*

Theodore Epp

❧ *Be to the world a sign that while we as Christians do
not have all the answers, we do know and care about the
questions.*

Billy Graham

BIG DREAMS

A thief comes to steal and kill and destroy,
but I came to give life—life in all its fullness.

John 10:10 NCV

    ⁖ Are you excited about the opportunities of today and thrilled by the possibilities of tomorrow? Do you confidently expect God to lead you to a place of abundance, peace, and joy? And, when your days on earth are over, do you expect to receive the priceless gift of eternal life? If you trust God's promises, and if you have welcomed God's Son into your heart, then you believe that your future is intensely and eternally bright.

    It takes courage to dream big dreams. You will discover that courage when you do three things: accept the past, trust God to handle the future, and make the most of the time He has given you today. No dreams are too big for God—not even yours. So start living—and dreaming—accordingly.

⁖ *You cannot out-dream God.*

John Eldredge

⁖ *The future lies all before us. Shall it only be a slight advance upon what we usually do? Ought it not to be a bound, a leap forward to altitudes of endeavor and success undreamed of before?*

Annie Armstrong

LIFE ETERNAL

*In a little while the world will not see me anymore,
but you will see me. Because I live, you will live, too.*

John 14:19 NCV

❧ Ours is a God who understands—far better than we ever could—the essence of what it means to be human. How marvelous it is that God became a man and walked among us. Had He not chosen to do so, we might feel removed from a distant Creator. But ours is not a distant God.

God understands our hopes, our fears, and our temptations. He understands what it means to be angry and what it costs to forgive. He knows the heart, the conscience, and the soul of every person who has ever lived, including you. And God has a plan of salvation that is intended for you. Accept it. Accept God's gift through the person of His Son Christ Jesus, and then rest assured: God walked among us so that you might have eternal life; amazing though it may seem, He did it for you.

❧ *If you are a believer, your judgment will not determine your eternal destiny. Christ's finished work on Calvary was applied to you the moment you accepted Christ as Savior.*

Beth Moore

ON BEYOND FAILURE

There is a time for everything, and everything on earth has its special season. There is a time to cry and a time to laugh. There is a time to be sad and a time to dance.

Ecclesiastes 3:1, 4 NCV

„ The occasional disappointments and failures of life are inevitable. There is simply no way around it—you will experience your fair share of setbacks that, by the way, are simply the price that you must occasionally pay for your willingness to take risks as you follow your dreams. But even when you encounter bitter disappointments, you must never lose hope.

Whenever we encounter the difficulties of life, God stands ready to protect us. Our responsibility, of course, is to ask Him for protection. When we call upon Him in heartfelt prayer, He will answer—in His own time and according to His own plan—and He will heal us. And, while we are waiting for God's plans to unfold and for His healing touch to restore us, we can be comforted in the knowledge that our Creator can overcome any obstacle, even if we cannot.

„ *Every misfortune, every failure, every loss may be transformed. God has the power to transform all misfortunes into "God-sends."*

Mrs. Charles E. Cowman

THE LAST WORD

For God has not given us a spirit of fear, but of power and of love and of a sound mind.

2 Timothy 1:7 NKJV

€ All of us may find our courage tested by the inevitable disappointments and tragedies of life. After all, ours is a world filled with uncertainty, hardship, sickness, and danger. Trouble, it seems, is never too far from the front door.

When we focus upon our fears and our doubts, we may find many reasons to lie awake at night and fret about the uncertainties of the coming day. A better strategy, of course, is to focus not upon our fears, but instead upon our God.

God is your shield and your strength; you are His forever. So don't focus your thoughts upon the fears of the day. Instead, trust God's plan and His eternal love for you. And remember: God is good, and He has the last word.

€ *Fear is a self-imposed prison that will keep you from becoming what God intends for you to be.*

Rick Warren

€ *Only believe, don't fear. Our Master, Jesus, always watches over us, and no matter what the persecution, Jesus will surely overcome it.*

Lottie Moon

IN THE FOOTSTEPS OF JESUS

Whoever serves me must follow me.
Then my servant will be with me everywhere I am.
My Father will honor anyone who serves me.

John 12:26 NCV

⁊ Whom will you walk with today? Will you walk with people who worship the ways of the world? Or will you walk with the Son of God? Jesus walks with you. Are you walking with Him? Hopefully, you will choose to walk with Him today and every day of your life. God's Word promises that when you follow in Christ's footsteps, you will learn how to live freely and lightly (Matthew 11:28-30).

If we are to be disciples of Christ, we must trust Him and place Him at very center of our beings. Jesus never comes "next." He is always first. The wonderful paradox, of course, is that it is only by sacrificing ourselves to Him that we gain eternal salvation.

Do you seek to fulfill God's purpose for your life? Then follow Christ. Follow Him by picking up His cross today and every day that you live. Then, you will quickly discover that Christ's love has the power to change everything, including you.

⁊ *A disciple is a follower of Christ. That means you take on His priorities as your own. His agenda becomes your agenda. His mission becomes your mission.*

Charles Stanley

HEEDING GOD'S CALL

One thing I do, forgetting those things which are behind
and reaching forward to those things which are ahead,
I press toward the goal for the prize of the upward call
of God in Christ Jesus.

Philippians 3:13-14 NKJV

⋯ It is vitally important that you heed God's call. In John 15:16, Jesus says, "You did not choose Me, but I chose you and appointed you that you should go and bear fruit, and that your fruit should remain, that whatever you ask the Father in My name He may give you" (NKJV). In other words, you have been called by Christ, and now, it is up to you to decide precisely how you will answer.

Have you already found your special calling? If so, you're a very lucky person. If not, keep searching and keep praying until you discover it. And remember this: God has important work for you to do—work that no one else on earth can accomplish but you.

⋯ *When God calls a person, He does not repent of it. God does not, as many friends do, love one day and hate another; or as princes, who make their subjects favorites and afterwards throw them into prison. This is the blessedness of a saint: his condition admits of no alteration. God's call is founded on His decree, and His decree is immutable. Acts of grace cannot be reversed. God blots out his people's sins, but not their names.*

Thomas Watson

GOD IS LOVE

*And we have known and believed the love that God
has for us. God is love, and he who abides in love
abides in God, and God in him.*

1 John 4:16 NKJV

❦ The Bible makes this promise: God is love.
It's a sweeping statement, a profoundly important
description of what God is and how God works.
God's love is perfect. When we open our hearts to His
perfect love, we are touched by the Creator's hand,
and we are transformed.

Today, even if you can only carve out a few quiet
moments, offer sincere prayers of thanksgiving to
your Creator. He loves you now and throughout all
eternity. Open your heart to His presence and His
love.

❦ *The life of faith is a daily exploration of the constant
and countless ways in which God's grace and love are
experienced.*

Eugene Peterson

❦ *Joy is the heart's harmonious response to the Lord's
song of love.*

A. W. Tozer

TRANSCENDENT LOVE

Who shall separate us from the love of Christ?
Shall tribulation, or distress, or persecution, or famine,
or nakedness, or peril, or sword? Yet in all these things
we are more than conquerors through Him who loved us.

Romans 8:35, 37 NKJV

❧ Where can we find God's love? Everywhere. God's love transcends space and time. It reaches beyond the heavens, and it touches the darkest, smallest corner of every human heart. When we become passionate in our devotion to the Father, when we sincerely open our minds and hearts to Him, His love does not arrive "some day"—it arrives immediately.

Today, take God at His word and welcome His Son into your heart. When you do, God's transcendent love will surround you and transform you, now and forever.

❧ *The grace of God transcends all our feeble efforts to describe it. It cannot be poured into any mental receptacle without running over.*

Vance Havner

❧ *Praise the Father for his loving kindness; tenderly cares He for His erring children. Praise Him.*

Elizabeth R. Charles

INFINITE POSSIBILITIES

Is anything too hard for the Lord?

Genesis 18:14 NKJV

ଽ Ours is a God of infinite possibilities. But sometimes, because of limited faith and limited understanding, we wrongly assume that God cannot or will not intervene in the affairs of mankind. Such assumptions are simply wrong.

Are you afraid to ask God to do big things in your life? Is your faith threadbare and worn? If so, it's time to abandon your doubts and reclaim your faith in God's promises.

God's Holy Word makes it clear: absolutely nothing is impossible for the Lord. And since the Bible means what it says, you can be comforted in the knowledge that the Creator of the universe can do miraculous things in your own life and in the lives of your loved ones. Your challenge, as a believer, is to take God at His word, and to expect the miraculous.

ଽ *We will see more and more that we are chosen not because of our ability, but because of the Lord's power, which will be demonstrated in our not being able.*

Corrie ten Boom

ଽ *So God's patience is His power over Himself. Great is that God who, having all power, yet keeps all power subject to Himself.*

Jim Elliot

HOPE IS CONTAGIOUS

*Finally, all of you be of one mind,
having compassion for one another; love as brothers,
be tenderhearted, be courteous.*

1 Peter 3:8 NKJV

  One of the reasons that God placed you here on earth is so that you might become a beacon of encouragement to the world. As a faithful follower of the One from Galilee, you have every reason to be hopeful, and you have every reason to share your hopes with others. When you do, you will discover that hope, like other human emotions, is contagious.

As a follower of Christ, you are instructed to choose your words carefully so as to build others up through wholesome, honest encouragement (Ephesians 4:29). So look for the good in others and celebrate the good that you find. As the old saying goes, "When someone does something good, applaud—you'll make two people happy."

  One of the ways God refills us after failure is through the blessing of Christian fellowship. Just experiencing the joy of simple activities shared with other children of God can have a healing effect on us.

Anne Graham Lotz

HELPING NEIGHBORS IN NEED

Let each of us please his neighbor for his good,
leading to edification.

Romans 15:2 NKJV

❧ Who are our neighbors? Jesus answered that question with the story of the Good Samaritan. Our neighbors are any people whom God places in our paths, especially those in need.

We know that we are instructed to love our neighbors, and yet there's so little time…and we're so busy. No matter. As Christians, we are commanded by our Lord and Savior to love our neighbors just as we love ourselves. Period.

This very day, you will encounter someone who needs a word of encouragement, or a pat on the back, or a helping hand, or a heartfelt prayer. And, if you don't reach out to that person, who will? If you don't take the time to understand the needs of your neighbors, who will? If you don't love your brothers and sisters, who will? So, today, look for a neighbor in need…and then do something to help. Father's orders.

❧ *The truest help we can render an afflicted man is not to take his burden from him, but to call out his best energy, that he may be able to bear the burden himself.*

Phillips Brooks

A LIFE OF INTEGRITY

He who walks with integrity walks securely,
But he who perverts his ways will become known.

Proverbs 10:9 NKJV

❧ As believers in Christ, we must seek to live each day with discipline, honesty, and faith. When we do, at least two things happen: integrity becomes a habit, and God blesses us because of our obedience to Him. Charles Swindoll correctly observed, "Nothing speaks louder or more powerfully than a life of integrity." Godly men and women agree.

Integrity is built slowly over a lifetime. It is a precious thing—difficult to build but easy to tear down.

Living a life of integrity isn't always the easiest way, but it is always the right way. And God clearly intends that it should be our way, too.

❧ *God never called us to naïveté. He called us to integrity.... The biblical concept of integrity emphasizes mature innocence not childlike ignorance.*

Beth Moore

❧ *The man who cannot believe in himself cannot believe in anything else. The basis of all integrity and character is whatever faith we have in our own integrity.*

Roy L. Smith

HIS VOICE

Fear not, for I am with you; Be not dismayed,
for I am your God. I will strengthen you,
Yes, I will help you, I will uphold you
with My righteous right hand.

Isaiah 41:10 NKJV

☣ Sometimes God speaks loudly and clearly. More often, He speaks in a quiet voice—and if you are wise, you will be listening carefully when He does. To do so, you must carve out quiet moments each day to study His Word and sense His direction.

Can you quiet yourself long enough to listen to your conscience? Are you attuned to the subtle guidance of your intuition? Are you willing to pray sincerely and then to wait quietly for God's response. Hopefully so. Usually God refrains from sending His messages on stone tablets or city billboards. More often, He communicates in subtler ways. If you sincerely desire to hear His voice, you must listen carefully, and you must do so in the silent corners of your quiet, willing heart.

☣ *Half an hour of listening is essential except when one is very busy. Then, a full hour is needed.*

St. Francis of Sales

THE WISDOM OF MODERATION

Patience is better than strength.
Controlling your temper is better than capturing a city.

Proverbs 16:32 NCV

🕉 Would you like to improve your life? Then harness your appetites and restrain your impulses. Moderation and wisdom are traveling companions. If we are wise, we must learn to temper our appetites, our desires, and our impulses. When we do, we are blessed, in part, because God has created a world in which temperance is rewarded and intemperance is inevitably punished.

Moderation is difficult, of course; it is especially difficult in a prosperous society such as ours. But the rewards of moderation are numerous and long-lasting. Claim those rewards today. No one can force you to moderate your appetites. The decision to live temperately (and wisely) is yours and yours alone. And so are the consequences.

🕉 *We are all created differently. We share a common need to balance the different parts of our lives.*

Dr. Walt Larimore

🕉 *If thou would be happy, have an indifference for more than what is sufficient.*

William Penn

UNBENDING TRUTH

Therefore, putting away lying,
"Let each one of you speak truth with his neighbor,"
for we are members of one another.

Ephesians 4:25 NKJV

&❦ We live in a world that presents us with countless temptations to wander far from God's path. These temptations have the potential to destroy us, in part, because they cause us to be dishonest with ourselves and with others.

Dishonesty is a habit. Once we start bending the truth, we're likely to keep bending it. A far better strategy, of course, is to acquire the habit of being completely forthright with God, with other people, and with ourselves.

Honesty, like its opposite, is also a habit, a habit that pays powerful dividends for those who place character above convenience. So, the next time you're tempted to bend the truth—or to break it—ask yourself this simple question: "What does God want me to do?" Then listen carefully to your conscience. When you do, your actions will be honorable, and your character will take care of itself.

&❦ *Learning God's truth and getting it into our heads is one thing, but living God's truth and getting it into our characters is quite something else.*

Warren Wiersbe

CONSTANT PRAISE

So through Jesus let us always offer to God our sacrifice of praise, coming from lips that speak his name.

Hebrews 13:15 NCV

✌ The Bible makes it clear: it pays to praise God. But sometimes, we allow ourselves to become so preoccupied with the demands of daily life that we forget to say "Thank You" to the Giver of all good gifts.

Worship and praise should be a part of everything we do. Otherwise, we quickly lose perspective as we fall prey to the demands of the moment.

Do you sincerely desire to be a worthy servant of the One who has given you eternal love and eternal life? Then praise Him for who He is and for what He has done for you. Praise Him all day long, every day, for as long as you live . . . and then for all eternity.

✌ *Praise God from whom all blessings flow. Praise Him all creatures here below. Praise Him above ye heavenly host. Praise Father, Son, and Holy Ghost.*

Thomas Ken

✌ *Praise—lifting up our heart and hands, exulting with our voices, singing his praises—is the occupation of those who dwell in the kingdom.*

Max Lucado

HE RENEWS OUR STRENGTH

Have you not known? Have you not heard?
The everlasting God, the Lord, the Creator of the ends of
the earth, neither faints nor is weary. His understanding
is unsearchable. He gives power to the weak, and to
those who have no might He increases strength.

Isaiah 40:28–29 NKJV

❧ Are you almost too weary to lift your head? Then bow it. When we genuinely lift our hearts and prayers to God, He renews our strength. Offer your concerns and your fears to your Father in Heaven. He is always at your side, offering His love and His strength.

Are you troubled or anxious? Take your anxieties to God in prayer. Are you weak or worried? Delve deeply into God's Holy Word and sense His presence in the quiet moments of the day. Are you spiritually exhausted? Call upon fellow believers to support you, and call upon Christ to renew your spirit and your life. Your Savior will never let you down. To the contrary, He will always lift you up if you ask Him to. So what, dear friend, are you waiting for?

❧ *God is not running an antique shop! He is making all things new!*

Vance Havner

❧ *He is the God of wholeness and restoration.*

Stormie Omartian

So Many Temptations

*No temptation has overtaken you except such as is
common to man; but God is faithful, who will not
allow you to be tempted beyond what you are able,
but with the temptation will also make the way of escape,
that you may be able to bear it.*

1 Corinthians 10:13 NKJV

❧ Have you noticed that this world is filled to the brim with temptations? Unless you've been living the life of a hermit, you've observed that temptation, both great and small, are everywhere.

Some temptations are small; eating a second scoop of ice cream, for example, is tempting, but not very dangerous. Other temptations, however, are not nearly so harmless. The devil is working 24/7, and he's causing pain and heartache in more ways than ever before. Thankfully, in the battle against Satan, we are never alone. God is always with us, and He gives us the power to resist temptation whenever we ask Him for the strength to do so.

In a letter to believers, Peter offered a stern warning: "Your adversary the devil walks about like a roaring lion, seeking whom he may devour" (1 Peter 5:8 NKJV). As Christians, we must take that warning seriously, and we must behave accordingly.

❧ *The devil's most devilish when respectable.*

Elizabeth Barrett Browning

THE SOURCE OF WISDOM

He who walks with wise men will be wise,
but the companion of fools will be destroyed.

Proverbs 13:20 NKJV

℣ The great English preacher, Charles Haddon Spurgeon, once wrote, "Wisdom is the right use of knowledge. To know is not to be wise. Many men know a great deal, and are all the greater fools for it. But to know how to use knowledge is to have wisdom." Spurgeon was, indeed, a very wise man.

To become wise, we must seek God's wisdom and live according to His Word. And, we must not only learn the lessons of the Christian life, we must also live by them.

Do you seek to live a life of righteousness and wisdom? If so, you must study the ultimate source of wisdom: the Word of God. You must seek out worthy mentors and listen carefully to their advice. You must associate, day in and day out, with godly men and women. And, you must act in accordance with your beliefs. When you do these things, you will become wise . . . and you will be a blessing to your friends, to you family, and to the world.

℣ *Wisdom is the foundation, and justice is the work without which a foundation cannot stand.*

St. Ambrose

SEVEN-DAY WORSHIP

All the earth shall worship You And sing praises to You;
They shall sing praises to Your name.

Psalm 66:4 NKJV

& If you really want to know God, you must be willing to worship Him seven days a week, not just on Sunday.

God has a wonderful plan for your life, and an important part of that plan includes the time that you set aside for praise and worship. Every life, including yours, is based upon some form of worship. The question is not whether you will worship, but what you worship.

If you choose to worship God, you will receive a bountiful harvest of joy, peace, and abundance. But if you distance yourself from God by foolishly worshiping earthly possessions and personal gratification, you're making a huge mistake. So do this: Worship God today and every day. Worship Him with sincerity and thanksgiving. Write His name on your heart and rest assured that He, too, has written your name on His.

& *I am of the opinion that we should not be concerned about working for God until we have learned the meaning and delight of worshipping Him.*

A. W. Tozer

A Time to Rest

Come to Me, all you who labor and are heavy laden,
and I will give you rest. Take My yoke upon you
and learn from Me, for I am gentle and lowly in heart,
and you will find rest for your souls.
For My yoke is easy and My burden is light.

Matthew 11:28-30 NKJV

⁖ God expects us to work hard, but He also intends for us to rest. When we fail to take the rest that we need, we do a disservice to ourselves and to our families. Sometimes, the struggles of life can drain us of our strength.

When we find ourselves tired, discouraged, or worse, there is a source from which we can draw the power needed to recharge our spiritual batteries. That source, of course, is God.

Is your spiritual battery running low? Is your energy on the wane? Are your emotions frayed? If so, it's time to turn your thoughts and your prayers to God. And when you're finished, it's time to rest.

⁖ *If we stay with the Lord, enduring to the end of His great plan for us, we will enjoy the rest that results from living in the kingdom of God.*

Serita Ann Jakes

THE GIFT OF TODAY

This is the day that the Lord has made.
Let us rejoice and be glad today!

Psalm 118:24 NCV

∞ For Christians, every day begins and ends with God and His Son. Christ came to this earth to give us abundant life and eternal salvation. We give thanks to our Maker when we treasure each day and use it to the fullest.

Today is God's gift to you. How you use it is your gift to God. So how do you plan to use today's gift? Will you celebrate God's blessings and obey His commandments? Will you share words of encouragement and hope with all who cross your path? Will you share the Good News of the risen Christ? Only you can answer these questions. May you answer wisely today and every day of your life.

∞ *With each new dawn, life delivers a package to your front door, rings your doorbell, and runs.*

Charles Swindoll

∞ *Today is mine. Tomorrow is none of my business. If I peer anxiously into the fog of the future, I will strain my spiritual eyes so that I will not see clearly what is required of me now.*

Elisabeth Elliot

OUR ULTIMATE HOPE

*And we have seen and testify that the Father
has sent the Son as Savior of the world.*

1 John 4:14 NKJV

❧ Christ is the ultimate Savior of mankind and the personal hope of those who believe in Him. Thomas Brooks spoke for believers of every generation when he observed, "Christ is the sun, and all the watches of our lives should be set by the dial of his motion." As His servants, we should place Him at the very center of our lives. And, every day that God gives us breath, we should share Christ's love and His message with a world that needs both.

❧ *Christ is no Moses, no exactor, no giver of laws, but a giver of grace, a Savior; he is infinite mercy and goodness, freely and bountifully given to us.*

Martin Luther

❧ *I now know the power of the risen Lord! He lives! The dawn of Easter has broken in my own soul! My night is gone!*

Mrs. Charles E. Cowman

❧ *Jesus be mine forever, my God, my heaven, my all.*

C. H. Spurgeon

REFLECTIONS

REFLECTIONS

REFLECTIONS

REFLECTIONS

REFLECTIONS

_____

_____

_____

_____

_____

_____

_____

_____

_____

_____

_____

_____

_____

_____

_____

_____

_____

_____

_____

_____

_____

_____

_____

REFLECTIONS

REFLECTIONS

_____

_____

_____

_____

_____

_____

_____

_____

_____

_____

_____

_____

_____

_____

_____

_____

_____

_____

_____

_____

_____

_____

_____

REFLECTIONS

_____

_____

_____

_____

_____

_____

_____

_____

_____

_____

_____

_____

_____

_____

_____

_____

_____

_____

_____

_____

_____

_____

REFLECTIONS

REFLECTIONS